RUGGED GIRL

A Memoir of Self-Destruction and the Journey to Freedom

Simone Alex

www.simonealex.com

Rugged Girl: A Memoir of Self-Destruction and the Journey to Freedom

Scripture quotation marked NKJV are from the New King James Version®. Copyright © 1982 by Thomas Nelson. Used by permission. All rights reserved.

Scripture quotation marked TPT are from The Passion Translation®. Copyright © 2017, 2018 by Passion & Fire Ministries, Inc. Used by permission. All rights reserved. www.thepassiontranslation.com

ISBN: 9781660816309

Cover design by Gabriel Watkins (gabewatkins@gmail.com)

Edited by Alyson Andrasik, Lauren Nanson, and Jaime Lynn Fusco

DEDICATION

This book is dedicated to Jesus, Who gave His life so that I could be free. Without Him, I would be dead.

To my loving parents, who have loved me in the best way that they know how and have done a wonderful job at that! They laid a firm foundation for me, even in all my years of turmoil. You made the "Rugged Girl" I am today. I am looking forward to many more years of hiking and skiing with you.

Thank you also to Troy, who loves me in spite of my past, just like Jesus does. I'm growing to love you more and more each day and that is the beauty of our journey together.

I'm in deep appreciation of my friends who have supported me on this journey, especially Chris and Colette, Shannon and Gabe, and Jaime.

To Bob and Dannah, thank you for giving me a platform to share this story early on in my walk with Jesus. Had you not trusted both God and me with your ministry, I would not have been able to write this book.

Without any of you at any point of my journey, I would not be here today. Your support has meant the world to me and you have honored the Lord through your love.

ENDORSEMENTS FOR RUGGED GIRL: A MEMOIR

I have had the privilege of knowing Simone for several years now. She is a talented woman who exhibits love and passion for others, for life and for her heavenly Father. While reading her life journey and testimony, I have grown to love and respect her even more.

In this book, Simone has captured and written her story which is full of the true and harsh realities of what can occur in a world where there is darkness and sin. But the great beauty she reveals is how the Lord came into her life and brought her salvation. A Savior, Who transformed and healed her from trauma and empowered her to overcome addiction. Simone is an overcomer.

If you have experienced trauma, emotional pain, depression, addiction in your past or are experiencing it now, this message will bring to you the truth and hope that Jesus has made available to you through the gift salvation. Through His forgiving and healing love, redemption and freedom is a beautiful gift and promise that will transform your life. He wants to heal you and set you free. Thank you, Simone for this transparent message that shows a life saved, rescued, and delivered into the freedom and victory Jesus has made available to all.

-Rebecca Greenwood

Co-Founder of Christian Harvest International

Author of *Let Our Children Go, Breaking the Bonds of Evil, Defeating Strongholds of the Mind, Your Kingdom Come, Glory Warfare*

Rugged Girl is a book that many women can relate to, including me. Simone does a great job leading you on an authentic journey of how one destructive root can alter your life and take you down a path that you'd never imagine. I love where Simone writes, "My pain followed me to every zip code and through every professional pursuit,". Having worked with many people in my coaching career, I've seen it play out where people haven't healed from deep wounds and are looking for a quick fix. We often want to run from pain or find an outward circumstance to heal an inward wound. This only continues the cycle of destruction as Simone so vibrantly illustrates in her book.

If you have gone through anything traumatic or feel as though you are on a hamster wheel of self-destruction, I highly recommend this book. You will learn that life can get better, life can be better, and when it is better, you might slide back to old ways, but you learn not to stay there. This book will show you what happens when struggle intersects with grace and how God is always waiting with open arms. If you are feeling discouraged, alone, hopeless, or ashamed, I encourage you to read this book because it will make you want to get up and fight like the Rugged Girl you are.

-*Tara Armstrong*

Life Coach and Founder of *She Shifts Culture* www.SheShiftsCulture.org

As you read through Rugged Girl you will see Simone's heart on these pages. Her desire to help others know that there is light on the other end of the tunnel is what has allowed her to be completely open, transparent and honest about her story that the vulnerability itself is what grips you and pulls you in. If you or someone you know has ever struggled with trauma, addiction, or finding that place where you belong in this world, then this story is an empowering testimony that will show you that not only can you survive, but you too can be an overcomer and emerge from that tunnel full of life!

-Jaime Lynn Fusco
President of The Wings of Destiny and CEO of New Moon Films

FOREWARD

I have personally known Simone Alex over the course of 9 years as she attended our church in West Hollywood that my husband, Jonathan and I Co-Pastor. Through the years, it has been evident that God's hand is clearly on Simone's life. Although I was unaware of the details of her life that are shared in depth in this memoir, I have always known Simone's strength came from a deep place of having found the God of her salvation. She knows who He is and whose she belongs to.

As a Pastor and the Founder of an organization that fights human trafficking, the question that continually comes up is "how" do the young ladies find themselves on a path that is clearly set for destruction? Although Simone is not a victim of human trafficking, her journey could've easily led her down a path where many girls I have counseled have tragically ended up. The story always begins with a tragic event of abuse that puts the young lady on a trajectory of vulnerability, often leading her to more abuse. In the case of Simone, the tragic event in her young life in which she details with courage set her on a path of self-destruction and of cycles of addiction and abuse.

The story she tells may not be foreign in this current generation where culture has glorified sex and drugs without revealing the truth of its tragic consequences. Many have walked a similar road, but Simone has bravely risen up to share the depth, the details, and the tragedies of her life without holding back. Her reason? Simply because she has a mandate to help others overcome as she herself has overcome.

The Simone I have come to know in the last 9 years is a woman of strength, courage, and determination. She is not absent from struggles, but she has learned to find strength in the God of her salvation. As with those who have struggled immensely with body image, substance abuse, or sexual immorality- everyday can be a fight to win. No matter where you might find yourself in your personal journey, YOU are not alone. Battles are won with the hope of victory in sight. It is my belief that many will find hope for themselves, or for loved ones who face a similar fight through the pages you now hold in your hand. You are not alone, and you can surely overcome.

"Through God, we will gain the victory" (Psalms 60:12)

-Sharon Ngai
Co-Pastor, Radiance International Hollywood House of Prayer
Founder, Justice Speaks

An Introduction

I've struggled for the last five years to write this book. I have wrestled with how to tell my story and the very question of why you, the reader, would want to read it. During this time, my life has been ever evolving, but my testimony remains the same. I've tried to shake the burning fire in my belly to share it and finally, after hours, days, and months of thinking, praying, talking over the story with my close friends, typing, rewriting, and edits too endless to count, here it is.

Writing this book has been like birthing a baby. Well, I've never actually birthed a baby. But if I had, I'd imagine that it would feel something like this, because my life was coming out of me on these pages. I've poured my heart out, been honest and raw with you, been transparent. I'm not trying to hide what's really happened over the years, because that's fake. I want to be real, because I know I'm not alone. Many women (and men) struggle in the same ways I have. We've all had hurts, pains, addictions and the like. I want to invite you to join me as I journey through my past, back into the trenches of what was, at times, warfare. In doing so, you will also learn how I survived those battles and stayed perpetually fighting in others.

We aren't always shown the battles that led to the victories in this Facebook and Instagram world we live in. We see mostly happy faces and the successes of everybody else's lives, rather than the real story behind the alluring smile, the sexy pose or the eloquent post. Our society has, in fact, been "selfie-ing" (my made-up word) for some time now and I think it's cultivated an environment where, "everything is fine, I'm just peachy keen, no problems here." It harkens back to the 1950s idea of "Leave It To Beaver" in which there was a picture perfect family and everything was just "swell." It wasn't an accurate portrayal of life then just as social media is not always an accurate portrayal of life now. I believe our society longs for transparency: from ourselves and from others.

It is also my hope, as you read my words of vulnerability, that you will realize that you aren't alone in your struggles. My life has not always been an easy road, but whose is? I believe that it's the very act of us sharing our stories with each other that makes us not feel so lonely in the turmoil, gives us a sense of hope. In so many ways, writing this book brought a lot of healing to my heart, but it is my prayer that while you read it, yours will be healed as well.

This book isn't just for women– these pervasive problems in our society affect both sexes. But because I am a woman, I have learned that the kinds of struggles I'm going to share with you are all too common amongst us. They all fall within the question of our identity and the value we place on ourselves. I'm going to take you back into the difficult memories of sexual assault, body image issues, destructive behaviors, and the like.

I became a working actor and model at a young age and my success did not bring immunity to these issues, but in most instances, made them worse. The glitz and glamour you see in photos and advertisements don't tell the real story, folks. In spite of a life of Hollywood, traveling the world, living in glamorous cities, and wearing some of the finest clothing money can buy, I struggled with everything many of my readers have. It is in these pages that I will pull back the veil, so that you can see the true faces of Simone: the good, the bad, and sometimes the ugly.

We are all in different phases of metamorphosis, being shaped and molded into something even more glorious than the previous version of who we were. The Word of God says we are going from glory to glory (2 Corinthians 3:18), and that "...the sufferings of this present time are not worthy to be compared with the glory which shall be revealed in us. For the earnest expectation of the creation earnestly waits for the revealing of the sons of God" (Romans 8:18-19 NKJV). This glory is a good enough reason for me to keep going, to keep getting out of bed every morning, to keep fighting the good fight of faith. That's why I'm laying out some basic weapons from my fight for you to pick and use in your own journey toward transformation and into a wide-open terrain of freedom.

Chapter 1

Rugged: "presenting a severe test of ability, stamina, or resolution; strongly built or constituted"

My dad and I used to roughhouse when I was little. I had to google that word, because he used it so much, I thought he had made it up. We make up words in our family and still use them when we communicate today. More on that later. Anyway, to roughhouse means to be rough and violent, like little boys are when they play. As it was with my dad and me. We would roughhouse and, as the last of three daughters, I figured it was his way of getting a little bit of the experience of having a boy. This was fine by me, as I was a pretty gritty, tough girl as far as I can remember.

We played football and every now and then, he'd let me get a touchdown, but there was a lot of tackling to get there. We wrestled. We played a made-up game called "jelly jump-ups" (he later told me that he named the game after a kind of pop-tart breakfast treat that was popular in the 1970's). Dad would throw a pillow at my feet and if I jumped and cleared it, I would get a point, but if I fell, he'd get a point. It was all in fun and love and it bred a perfectly balanced tomboy, one moment wrestling and playing football with my dad, another moment playing with Barbies in the bathtub or putting on make-up in the mirror. I also don't remember anyone ever telling me, "You're a girl" or "You're a boy," I just was.

It was the 1970s and Wonder Woman was my favorite superhero. I had a Wonder Woman bathing suit, Underoos, and a Charlie's Angels lunch box. I wanted special powers so that I could conquer big feats. Nothing seemed impossible. I operated in a world of make believe like most children do. My main "gig" in this pretend world was performing, and my main "stage" was my parents' stone hearth in front of their fireplace in the living room. It was there that I gave some of my best singing and dancing performances. Then I'd put on a matching satin outfit that had the words "Roller Disco" on the front, lace up my roller skates, turn off all the lights save one or two, and boogie to the Saturday Night Fever Soundtrack across my parent's linoleum floors. I also pretended I was an Olympic athlete in gymnastics (on a short balance beam we owned) or was playing tennis in the finals at Wimbledon (hitting a ball off the side of the house for hours on end). My life was based on one big imaginary scenario of my make-believe world.

My childhood shenanigans are the plots for stories that are still being told, like the infamous tale of me repeatedly locking myself in the bathroom for hours on end while I sold soap and toothpaste in the mirror (think commercial actress in the making). My mom would leave me in the bathtub while I lathered my hair with bubbles explaining to a pretend camera about the benefits of the next new shampoo and how they would make someone's hair look as luscious and full like that of Farrah Fawcett. She'll tell you that she would come in and check on me in the tub from time to time to see if my fingers and toes were getting wrinkled like prunes from being waterlogged.

I lived across town from the elementary school I attended, which meant that I didn't know many kids in my neighborhood. My two sisters were five and eleven years older than me, so they were spending time with friends their own age. There was not much left for me to do but play alone. I didn't realize it at the time, but I was very lonely. I felt like an outsider when I was at school and when I was at home, but in what would become true Simone fashion, I would shrug it off and press on.

It was the late '70s and early '80s when kids were still being "kids" without the influence of social media, video games or internet videos. This meant getting dirty on a swing set, riding our Big Wheels or playing hopscotch in the driveway outlined with chalk. I would drift off into my imaginary world and used my creativity to entertain myself. I pretended I was in soap operas, commercials, that I was a high fashion model, anything that had to do with performing on camera. My parents called me hyperactive, but now that I'm an adult, I realize that this was fairly normal childhood behavior. Each child is unique in their giftings, and I was clearly born a performer and an athlete.

The Simone of this era was a carefree kid and a naturally confident little girl. She was also a total goofball. When people had their eyes on me, I would make sure I was dramatic, expressive and silly just to make them smile and laugh. I was into boogers and farts and everything that was gross, making milk come out my nose or running into a bathroom stall to loudly announce what I found in the toilet: a born show off.

My dad was a university professor of geology, so every summer from the time I was six months old until about eight years old, my family traveled to a field school in the mountains of Utah where he would instruct a group of college students. It was there that I continued to hone my skills as an exhibitionist. At five or six years old, I walked into the hotel bar, climbed up on a table, and danced like a crazy person while all his students laughed.

Some of my earliest memories were out in the wilderness on these hiking trails in the Wasatch Mountains just outside of Salt Lake City. It was up amongst those rocky peaks that I felt the most free. It was also the closest to my parents that I'd ever felt. They would tuck me safely into their backpack (the ones that are made for toddlers to be carried in) and we would hike for days on end. When we returned to the ski lodge where we stayed, I'd jump in the pool and swim like a fish until my fingers would prune up, just like in the bathtub. One time, when I was around three years old, I broke free of my mom's hand and took off running as fast as my little legs could carry towards that pool with one goal in mind: jumping in. Suddenly, she burst out a blood curdling scream. I stopped dead in my tracks. Why? There was no water in the pool and I had been making a beeline straight for the deep end. My energy and determination knew no limits.

My parents taught me how to snow ski when I was three years old. They bundled me up in a snowsuit, strapped on tiny skis, and brought me to the top of a mountain at a local ski area. My mom would stand at one side of the hill and my dad would stand at the other side. I giggled with glee, as one would push me across to the other parent, then I would lay down, flip my skis over to point the other direction, and that parent would push me to the other side. This repeated over and over for close to an hour until my little toddler body got down that hill. Looking back on it today, it's a clear picture of them teaching me how to be rugged and independent. I could have gotten taken out by a fast paced skier while I was moving across that hill all alone. However, I kept my eyes on my loving parent who was patiently waiting for me to arrive to the other side. It was such a profound experience, that I remember it like it was yesterday.

I was not raised in a Christian home, nor did I know the story of the gospel or about Jesus. My parents view spirituality from a science background, so if a concept isn't proven, they lean towards disbelief. However, I did periodically attend Catholic Mass with my babysitter's family after a Saturday night sleepover. "Auntie Pat" would make her famous spaghetti (she was Italian) after the service and we'd all eat and feel fat and happy. Their family was very committed to their faith, and I believe that their devotion instilled a subtle hunger in me to learn more about God at a very early age. She truly exemplified the love of Christ to me.

Apparently, this family found me very entertaining, because they would spend endless hours being my audience. I even made them my guinea pigs for my "hair salon" when I would fake cut all of their hair into my made up hairstyle called a "pishwa" (I was constantly making up words). They would indulge me at my every whim, appreciating me in all of my silly quirkiness.

In 1984, my dad had a sabbatical year in Switzerland and my mom and I went to live with him for six months. It was one of the best experiences of my life. I soaked in every detail of the experience, from walking around medieval towns to skiing in the Alps, to traveling through Italy to the shores of Greece, then back to Paris to climb up the Eiffel Tower (more on that later).

I had been an artistic child, but this awakened something deeper, a hunger to be creative. I started drawing, designing fashion, making my own clothes, dancing (even more than I was before), and listening to all kinds of music (Tears for Fears was on repeat for the whole year). I was inspired by the diversity of languages in Europe that I stayed true to my love of making up words and developed my own five-word language. My family still uses it in their vernacular to this day.

My parents also allowed me to be independent. I remember taking the tram into downtown Basel and going into a department store to buy (said) Tears for Fears cassette tape. I had no fear that anything bad would happen to me. I was ten years old and I viewed the world as my oyster.

My "dancing career" continued when we spent a week in Greece at a luxury resort during a conference my father was attending. I heard about a talent show that the social director was arranging so of course I entered. What we didn't realize when I put my name on the list was that it was going to be held in a bar late at night. My parents went along with it anyway, and I set to work on preparing my dance routine to "Everybody Wants to Rule the World," by who else but Tears for Fears. Here I was at ten years old, stepping on stage to compete against people three times my age. Dad whipped out his massive camcorder and recorded the performance on VHS, which I still have to this day. The bar was filled with cigarette smoke and drunk patrons who paid little attention to the girl on stage. I tuned out the world as I danced my heart out in my element of performing.

I had started figure skating before we moved to Europe and picked it back up again right when we returned to the States. I was serious about it. All the focus and intensity I had put into the balance beam and a tennis racket in my "pretend world" was now being channeled onto the ice. It was a sport that I had been created for, a perfect combination of strength and art. I got to be the tough girl who had been bred through the years of wrestling and hiking and put that energy towards my powerful jumps. The artistic side of me adored dancing to my favorite music (Erasure and Metallica) on the ice. It was a beautiful outlet in my life as my competitive spirit was filled through training and competitions.

It was also after getting home from Switzerland that I started to see what was going on with boys. They were cute and the talk of all my friends. I was age eleven, and I was like a fish out of water with my new silver grill of braces and short feathered hair cut (it was 1985, folks). I think of her baby face now and it just squeezes my heart tight. I want to run back in time and save her from all the painful years that lay before her.

Chapter 2

Violated: "to break, disregard; to do harm to the person or especially the chastity of"

The summer before my seventh-grade year, my friend had a "brilliant" idea to set me up with a popular eighth grade boy. This was new to me. I had never been "set up" (if there even is such a thing at that young age). But she thought we might end up "going together." I made sure nothing was stuck in my braces, brushed my perfectly coiffed feathered hair and put on my best Opus the Penguin sweatshirt (a cartoon character from the comic strip "Bloom County"). It was appropriate for my age and represented my sense of humor and personality. I also cherished it because it was given to me by my babysitter's family. I thought everyone else would like it just as much and furthermore, like me in it. We set off for the local arcade.

When we walked in, here was this boy sporting a mullet and propped up on a video game machine waiting for us. The meeting was brief and then I went off to the bathroom leaving my friend with him. When I returned, she said, "Let's go." Once outside of the arcade I asked, "What did he say?" She said, "Do you really want to know?" To which I answered, "Yes!" Then she delivered the blow: "He said, 'No way!'" This may seem like your basic run-of-the-mill pre-teen scenario you might see in a Netflix series, but these words stung to my core. It was as if this boy's words rejected everything about me. All of the sudden I felt ugly, not only in my face, my teeth, my hair and my body, but also in my outfit that I so carefully chose. It was the first time I ever felt "not good enough," a lie that has chased me ever since.

It's been hard for me to define what the term "not good enough" means. In this particular situation, I believed I wasn't pretty enough or cool enough or even had enough of a personality for a boy to like me. I perceived that who Simone was wasn't sufficient for the world. And with each negative or painful event that happened to me, the lie became stronger. It was as if layers of dark paint were beginning to gloss over the innocent, joyful Simone. Not long after the incident at the arcade, she was barely recognizable.

I was at the zenith of my skating career. I'd just started to move into national competitions. My parents, coach, and I had just arranged for me to move 3 hours away to a Philadelphia superb to train with an Olympic coach. I was going for it. We were practicing for an ice skating show that was held yearly at our rink. I had one of the solo performances and was going to skate to "Phantom of the Opera".

I'd become a multi-purpose creative skater. I choreographed my own programs and designed my hand-made costumes. A group of skaters, including myself, were on the ice for practice for one of our group performances. Unbeknownst to me, as I was standing there listening to my coach with my left toe-pick resting in the ice, it froze. As soon as I moved to turn and go skate, my body went, but my toe stayed frozen. I fell. My knee went one way and my body went the other. It was some of the worst pain I had ever felt.

As I lay there writhing in pain on the ice, my skating dreams flashed before me and questions bombarded my mind. Would I be able to perform in the show? Would I be able to compete? Is my skating career over? About 20 minutes later, an ambulance drove onto the ice, the EMT's put me on a stretcher and placed me inside, then took me to the emergency room.

After a battery of tests, the doctor determined that I dislocated my knee and tore my meniscus cartilage, which holds my kneecap in place. He said I could come back from this injury, but I had to be immobile for several weeks and it would take months for me to recover. I would have to dedicate my free time to rehab and to working hard to regain my muscle strength to get back to my previous skill level.

It's very common for athletes to return from their injuries even better than before they fell. Most do make the choice to dedicate their time to fully recovery, no matter the cost. However, as I was laying in bed for weeks after the accident, gaining weight, immobile, on medication, I had a lot of time to think and make some big decisions. Performing in the skating show and moving away to train with the Olympic coach was definitely out of the question, at least for the time being. I then had to make a decision about my career and how committed I was to the sport.

I had become a pre-teen and then a teenager, I realized how lonely I had been training and competing, isolated from my school friends. I wanted to enjoy my life and experience what everyone else my age was experiencing. I longed to be a "normal" teenager. So when my parents sat me down and explained to me that skating was very expensive, and that I needed to make a definitive decision to continue to compete or to end my career, I chose to end it in hopes of a new life for myself.

Skating had been amazing, but I missed so many moments in junior high and my first year of high school. I'd wake up at 4:45am to be on the ice from 5:45am to 7:45am, then change and head to school. I'd be back again for an afternoon practice. In addition to that, I had a personal trainer that I worked out with at the gym two times a week. My life was serious about skating. It is a very individual sport and having spent a lot of time alone, I craved a social life. And when friends told stories at school of what they did the previous night or over the weekends, I always felt left out because I was at the rink.

For the previous seven years, my life revolved around skating. When I would tell people about myself or others would describe me, we would almost always include the description "figure skater". Now I was just Simone and as any teenager does, whether they realize it or not, I was trying to figure out who I was, where I fit into high school, and seek after other's approval. All of a sudden, I was trying to figure out who I was without skating in my life. I was searching for a new identity.

That summer, I hung out with friends nearly all of the time. I was trying to soak up the days, months and years that I had missed with them while I was skating. It was within the few months after the skating accident. We started drinking anything we could get our hands on: beer, vodka, whiskey, wine coolers, you name it. This was how we spent time together and when I got drunk, it was a release for me after all those years of being a disciplined athlete.

Our little parties would be at each other's houses long after our parents fell asleep, but it wasn't long before we were invited to a college party. We lived in a small town centered around a major university, so college parties were the norm for everyone we knew. This one was a "kegger". If you don't know what this kind of party is, it's where there are numerous metal kegs filled with nearly 16 gallons of beer laid out with the sole purpose of getting guests incredibly intoxicated. These parties are part of the college town life. It was this warm, summer night in August 1989 that my life took a sharp turn in a different direction.

My hair was long and curly brown, and because I had been a skater, I was still physically fit and healthy. I wore a blue and white checkered mini-skirt and a white t-shirt with blue writing from the Gap, hoping to look older than my age, so that I wouldn't be noticed for being too young to drink.

13

We arrived at the party in the tiny apartment of a downtown high rise. I was immediately given a 32-ounce super-sized plastic McDonald's cup which I promptly filled with beer. I didn't think much of my decision to drink that night, since we had been drinking all summer. All of my friends and everyone else at the party were doing the same thing.

We lived in a well-known university town, and this is what the high school and college students did for fun. Many of my friends had older siblings and friends who were over twenty-one, and it was common for them to head a few miles into town and attend one of these parties. What did we tell our parents? That we were going to hang out at the arcade (the same one where I had that fateful meeting with mullet-boy) or staying at a friend's house overnight. Much of the time, each of us would tell our parents that we were sleeping over at each other's house, but our parents would never cross-reference with each other, so our lies were safe.

That night, we were crammed in this one or two bedroom apartment with more people flooding in by the minute. Music was playing and I was guzzling down beer while chatting with friends when I noticed a man staring at me from across the room. I could tell that he was several years my senior, but as a 14 year old girl, I can't say that I minded the attention of an older man. I was flattered.

Eventually, he made his way across the room and started talking to me. I still remember the way his 1980's Tom Selleck mustache moved when he formed his words. We talked for a while and we figured out that he went to school with my older sister who was in her early 20's. I was getting drunker and I must have told him I was in high school, but his age didn't register to me in my foggy state. He said he was headed to another party and asked if I would I like to come. At this point, after several beers, I was light-headed, giddy and bit sick to my stomach, but nonetheless, I said yes. We took the elevator downstairs, climbed into the bed of a pickup truck and took off for the next party.

At this point, I was in a near blackout state and not conscious of the decisions I was making or what I was doing. In many ways, this state was a very freeing place to be, because I wasn't concerned about anything. Alcohol and being drunk took a load off of my shoulders after the trauma of the skating accident, which was on my mind every day. I didn't have to think about anything else than having fun. I was with my friends in my small hometown and I had no reason to trust that I wouldn't be safe.

As we were driving down the main drag in my hometown, I leaned over the back of the truck to vomit right out of the tailgate, but in front of the cars behind us. The man who had been staring at me all night was right at my side holding my hair back.

We didn't stay at the other party for long and were brought back to the original apartment complex where we started the night. This man was by my side the whole time. It had to be clear to anyone who came in contact with me that I was seriously drunk.

He took me under his wing that night, like a protective older brother or even someone who liked me, taking care of me in my inebriated state. My innocent mind reasoned that I was safe with him.

In the wee hours of the morning, he offered to walk me back to the place I was staying that night, which was only two blocks from the party. Halfway there he started to kiss me. I was young and inexperienced, so it was new and felt good. But then it took a turn and became heated.

I've spent years piecing together my memories of this story. Truth be told, for a lot of years I had erased the details from my memory, because I didn't want to remember it. I sit here writing this story 30 years later and the details come flooding back like they happened yesterday.

While we were making out heavily, I remember him clearly asking me if I wanted to "do this". I didn't fully understand what he was asking. My thoughts were not clear and my defenses were down.

When a person is drunk, all logical reasoning is thrown out the window. It's why people pick up their car keys, slide into the driver's seat, start the ignition, then drive down the road. In those foggy moments, we don't realize what the ramifications of our decision will be. Irrational choices are made.

That night, in my drunken state, I said, "Yes". One alcohol induced word changed my life forever. I lost my virginity on the grassy lawn of a Lutheran church in the heart of my hometown.

After that, I blacked out. My memory was simply erased from the alcohol. I don't remember how we left from there, but somehow we ended up in his apartment. When I woke up the next morning, my head was throbbing. He got up from the bed, out from under the bloody sheets, and that was the first time I had seen any man naked. I could hardly grasp what had transpired or comprehend who I was looking at. It scared me. He had a look of pride on his face. What had I done? I was horrified, disgusted, and completely and utterly ashamed.

He was 23 and I was just 14. It was statutory rape.

Wikipedia cites that statutory rape is defined in several different ways according to which city or state the crime occurred. It says, "different jurisdictions use many different terms for this crime, such as forcible sexual activity, in which one of the individuals is below the age of consent; rape of a child; corruption of a minor; unlawful sex with a minor or child sex abuse." In my case, there was a 9-year age difference.

I didn't know it was rape at the time. In fact, it took me years to realize what happened. It had to be clear to him that I was drunk when he "took care of me" throughout the episodes of vomiting, stumbling, and slurred words. Secondly, we live in a small town. The college students at that party knew that we were from the high school and after talking to this man about my older sister, he knew that I was too. Everybody there knew each other indirectly. Furthermore, now that I'm an adult and I see a 14-year-old girl, it is almost always apparent that she is underage. These are the details that I have had to go over and remind myself hundreds of times in my head over the years since, in order to eventually come to terms with the truth.

That fateful word "yes" that I had uttered on the grass that summer night consumed my mind. I had consented to sex, even though I did not understand what I was saying yes to or even what I was doing with my body while I was drunk.

I felt dirty, embarrassed, ashamed and depressed. The one thing that I held close to my heart and my body, that I had been saving for a special person in my future, was taken from me.

That morning, I put on my clothes and walked out of his apartment. I don't even remember how I got back to my parent's house, but I did. When I arrived, I was a remarkably different girl than the one who had left for the party the night before.

My life was suddenly upside down as I began my 10th grade year of high school. I'd wake up in the mornings crying. Within one month of the rape, I became apathetic and started to lose the energy and zest for life that had always characterized me. I was like a zombie, the walking dead. I could barely make it through my classes without breaking down in tears. I missed countless days of school. My parents thought that I had Chronic Fatigue Syndrome, because my zest for life had seeped out of me. I was lethargic. I didn't understand what was going on with me either and never connected the rape to how I was feeling.

I discovered that I could go to the guidance counselor's office at school. It became a safe reprieve for me during this time and almost every day of that year was marked by a visit to a certain counselor who would allow me to cry for hours on end. I never told her what happened just a few months prior, because it wasn't until years later that I made the connection between the rape and the hopelessness I was experiencing on a day to day basis.

The Fall of 1989 marked what I remember to be the beginning of a battle with depression. All of my dreams, passions, and bright spark of life that had marked my childhood and skating career were crushed and smothered as a result of the trauma. It was also the first time that I ever had thoughts of ending my life. I wanted to crawl out of my skin, as I was disgusted with myself, blamed myself, felt ashamed and dirty.

I didn't really grasp the magnitude of what had happened to me. I just hated who I was, my body and my life. It never occurred to me that this was my assailant's fault. I reasoned that it was my choice to drink that night, that I was dressed inappropriately and was somehow "too attractive". I had concluded that even in my drunken state I had consented to the sexual encounter, so therefore I was to blame for the way I was feeling and deserved every bit of the aftermath of it.

To make matters worse, the word about that night spread like wildfire throughout the high school. Of course, nobody knew the truth about what really happened. They assumed I chose to have sex with an older man, so they called me "slut" and word got around that I was "easy." That's a more juicy narrative to tell anyway.

It was like a big yellow post-it note that my peers were sticking to my back. When a person, especially a teenager, is trying to figure out her identity and where she fits into the world, it's not hard to believe what others are saying. So, I believed (and eventually assumed) the label given to me: slut.

Every teenager is at a critical juncture of figuring out who he or she is as an individual. For me, I had wanted to go to the Olympics and for several years of my childhood, defined myself as a competitive athlete. It was my foremost desire and my number one goal. That drive was what got me out of bed every school day at four a.m. to be at the rink for five a.m. practice. I was admired by my friends for my determination. But a few short months after my skating career ended, I was raped. So, on top of seeking to discover who I was without skating in my life, I was struggling to get through the trauma and figure out who exactly Simone was after this incident.

As the depression worsened, I turned to anything that might mask the pain. I started to go to more parties and drink alcohol with the goal of getting drunk. It was actually the only time during these dark days that the old, goofy Simone from my childhood would make a resurgence. The irony was that, even though being drunk caused me to let my guard down, which led to that fateful night, I still ran full force towards it.

When I was drunk, people would laugh at my silliness. It made me feel carefree. I felt loved by my friends. However, when I drank, I didn't run from sexual encounters, but towards them. Not a logical reaction, but by being sexually promiscuous, I was subconsciously taking on the label that not only my peers had given me, but that I had given myself.

I also believed that sex was all I was worth to a man. I so desperately wanted to be loved in this season of sadness. I felt so alone in what I was experiencing. In my backwards thinking, I thought that if I could trade sex for a man's comfort and affection, it would take my pain away. But I never found what I was looking for, and intimacy with a man always left me feeling emptier than I was the day before.

One story tells a picture of where my life was at this time. It sums up the depths of darkness I way lying in at the time. This occurred only a year or two after the rape and I have only shared this story with a few people in my life before writing this book. I'm here to be transparent, because there are so many out there who have had similar experiences and I want my readers to know just how bad things had gotten for me.

As I continued to go to college parties, I went to a house rented by a group of college guys one night. As was my normal mode of operation in those days, I got blackout drunk. I woke up naked in a stranger's bed. To this day, I don't know what exactly happened to me or who it happened with. But a friend of mine later explained that she had looked in and saw me with another man and possibly other men too, although she couldn't be sure.

It was like I was allowing my body to be thrown to the wolves and devoured.

I spiraled further into a cycle of self-destructive behavior. I was like a drunken rag doll tossed around from night to night, man to man, and I blamed myself for every incident I got myself into. The irony was that

I was allowing myself to be in these situations, even choosing them. How could I have not realized that going out to parties and drinking would only end up in the same way it had been time and again? At that point of my life, I didn't even think of trying to break free from it. Even if I had wanted to, I wouldn't have known how. I simply didn't know how to be anyone else but this party girl.

The rest of my high school years were a struggle with dating. There were those who thought I was pretty and good looking, yet others who heard the rumors that I was "easy" and would want to go out with me because they thought they could get sex. But guys' attraction to me was rarely, if ever, from a genuine, good place. Most were selfish and lustful. At least from what I can remember from my perspective. They didn't care about me, but what they could get from me. In a sense, they preyed on me, but I allowed them to. I didn't know who else to be but prey. I dressed sexier, put on coats of make-up and played the role as a vixen. But I couldn't keep up that façade for long.

If I did like a guy and get comfortable with him, I would begin to let my guard down and allow the bits and pieces of the real Simone to come out. Underneath all the of coping, I truly did want to find someone who I could trust and be vulnerable with. That meant talking, sharing, caring and everything that encompasses a relationship apart from the act of sex. The foundation of human connection.

Deep down inside, I wanted a man to like me for me, not for the person they heard I was, thought I was, or even the girl I pretended I was. This didn't go very well for me. When I connected with someone I liked and felt vulnerable enough to show my true colors, I started to open up (or the guy had sex with me, whichever came first), he would break up with me. I distinctly remember one of them saying to a friend of mine (who then repeated it to me), "when I found out she was a real person, it turned me off." Yet again, the message delivered to me was that guys wanted the outside of me, my body, and not the inside, real Simone.

As much as I tried to be accepted, I ended up being rejected time and again. The emotional pain during these teenage years grew like a cancer. It manifested in several different ways. I started to have issues with food and my weight. I had already been dieting off and on since I started figure skating, starting at the ripe old age of eight. However, after the skating accident, then the rape following it, depression hit my life and my weight started to increase dramatically.

My parents noticed a big change in my body, but they had no idea what I had just been through. We have always been a "weight conscious" family. If we were carrying extra pounds, it was a sign to us that we were unhealthy, so we always tried to deal with it through diet and exercise. My mom and dad surmised it was a good idea to take me to Weight Watchers meetings to learn tools to help control my weight. I felt like an alien in my flesh, so as much as I didn't want to go, I agreed to it.

Those were the days that they weighed you in front of everyone and it felt more like shaming than support. Nobody else in my high school went to Weight Watchers, but here I was struggling with alcohol, sexual abuse (as in, allowing myself to be abused) and now my body size. I was now wearing a new label: fat.

The weight loss program served to increase my sensitivity about my body at 15 years old. I was already self-conscious about my body given the trauma I had experienced. In fact, I hated it. I would try to fill the hole of despair with food. The more I knew I wasn't supposed to eat, the more I wanted.

Weight Watchers had a line of desserts that my parents would buy for me to help with the program. Little did they know I would eat the whole box late at night when nobody was watching. After binges like that made me feel bloated and sick to my stomach, I would starve myself. This cycle carried on through my days at school and at nights in my house. I felt emotionally and physically heavy. They went hand in hand.

The depression quickly led to suicidal thoughts. Every time I would hit a low point in my emotions, I would think about killing myself, specifically cutting my wrists. I'd think about how I would do it over and over again, yet I never attempted.

Looking back on these times, there was always just a sliver of hope, an ember of the fire of the real Simone somewhere deep down inside of me that kept me going. That girl who was full of life, passionate, silly, joyful, fun, creative, loving and carefree had to be inside of me somewhere. I must have known that she couldn't have been completely lost because she was there just a few years prior. I had to believe there was something or someone waiting for me on the other side of my darkness.

Chapter 3

Reverie: "living out a dream during the day; a daydream"

I slowly started to find my competitive drive again, particularly in other sports. I'd been lifting weights since I was ten years old and had enjoyed working out. When I would go to the gym, I would train hard. It was a place that I could let out my aggression and anger for what I was going through. It also helped my depression. It was 1990 and female fitness competitors and body builders were becoming popular.

The sport sparked my interest. I was strong and carried a lot of muscle on my frame, so I toyed with the idea of competing and looked into what it would take to become a success at it. I read muscle magazines to learn all the tricks of the trade. I had the workouts down and since I was already on a diet eating program with Weight Watchers, it seemed like I could transition into getting prepared for stage, but my issues with food and weight were becoming obsessive.

I was secretly binging on food and couldn't stop myself. Late at night, I'd sneak to the kitchen and eat as much as I could. It was temporarily filling a hole in the pit of my stomach. I'd eat an apple pie or leftover pizza, whatever else I could get my hands on to, then I'd go right to sleep. I had the desire to get back to being a healthy, fit competitor, but I couldn't stop myself. My binging was my way of coping with my pain. As long as I was unable to control my "secret eating" patterns, I was not going to be able to lean down my figure to compete as a bodybuilder. Rather than deal with my binging problem, I abandoned the idea of bodybuilding altogether.

During these years, every summer, my parents would take us boating and the whole family water-skied. About a year after I quit skating, we attended a slalom waterski school in Florida. I got excited, as I started to think about competing in this sport. It was fun and aggressive and I was good at it. But once we got back to my hometown, my personal battle continued to rage. I was wrestling with a lack of confidence that held me back like prison bars. I desperately wanted to get back to the Simone who existed just a few years prior. I wanted to excel at everything I put my hand to, but it was like I was paralyzed from moving forward, so my water-skiing career never got past a dream.

The high school years seemed to drag on for ages, but I pressed through them. After four years of floundering in my emotions, trying to get solid footing in my life and process what happened to me, I finally opened up about the rape. I wrote a poem about that night and read it at an open mic poetry event at a local cafe.

It was a bold public confession, especially in my small hometown, since everyone pretty much knew everyone else. Previously, I had never shared much with anyone the details that happened that summer when I was 14. But over the years, as the feelings continued to surface, I was desperate to express the emotions any way I could.

After I read the poem that night, the story spread like wildfire around town. What had been a public confession in an attempt to find healing, ended up becoming community gossip. I had never told my family about the rape, but they ended up finding out through a friend who attended the poetry night. My parents' reaction to the news that their daughter had been raped was very emotional, filled with disbelief, confusion and anger. I felt like the wound was opened up all over again. In my attempt to heal through my poem and my public confession, things had only gotten worse for me.

There's no clinical manual on how to help your child heal from sexual assault, at least not that I know of. My parents were processing the shocking information and trying to help the best way they knew how. They got me into counseling.

Seeing a therapist helped me verbally process what I was going through emotionally, but it was very clinical. He would ask questions and I would answer them for fifty minutes and then I would walk out of the office. This would be on repeat for weeks on end. I felt like a patient, as if there was something wrong with me that I even needed counseling at all. That made me feel even more like a victim.

I didn't need trauma to be dealt with in a cold therapist-patient relationship. I needed love. I needed to know that I was valued and that I was worthy of living. I needed to know the rape and all the behavior that I experienced afterwards wasn't my fault. The problem was, I didn't know what I needed at the time, so I couldn't verbalize it.

When my dog is hurting, she yelps, because she can't speak. As her mama, I scoop her up and try to do my very best to find out where the pain is, because she cannot articulate to me where it is and how it happened. If I can't find where she is hurting, I just hold her and love her until she is either better and over the pain or has to go to the vet. Either way, I choose to just love her and let her know she's not alone and that I'm here for her.

Like my dog, I couldn't express exactly where I was hurting, but needed arms wrapped around me to hold me and love me. However, because I was still processing through the pain, I couldn't express to others what would make me feel better. And even if I had, I'm not certain that those around me were capable of giving it to me at the time. Everybody is different in how they respond to crisis.

Since I didn't receive what I so desperately needed, I felt as though I had a tremendous lack of support for what I had gone through. This made me feel even more abandoned and lonely than ever before.

Shortly after the open mic night at the café, I got sick. It was just a normal respiratory infection that goes around in the winter, but mine went deep into my chest. I went to the doctor and he prescribed Prednisone, a steroid to open up my lungs to breathe better during the congestion. As I started to take the medication, I began to have sleepless nights. I spent hours awake as if I had just downed ten espressos. My painting and writing became more prolific. Details of the rape surfaced. I started to obsess over expressing myself. All my thoughts and emotions rushed to the surface with full intensity. I couldn't focus clearly, yet in a way, it's as clear as I had ever been able to see.

I felt like I was on a high, as if everything I'd gone through for the past few years was gushing out of me through words, writing, and painting. It was a stark contrast to the girl who had been depressed and sullen. All of a sudden, there was this intensity of expressing my pain and letting it all out.

For a couple of weeks, I was awake for days on end, pouring myself out into art. Because I wasn't sleeping well, I had gotten off cycle of taking the medication. It needed to be taken in a very specific way and tapered off closer to the end of the bottle. However, I did none of that, but rather took the same dose the whole way through. By the end of the bottle, on my last few days, my brain felt like the wires were being pulled out of it. I started to meltdown.

So much so, that it kept me awake at night. However, at the end of those two weeks, I started to crash. Depression, hopelessness, and suicidal thoughts took over my mind and body in those last few days. It was a dramatic contrast to what I'd just experienced. It was the highest of highs and the lowest of lows.

I had gotten to be friends with a few other girls who were going to college in my hometown. I needed someone to talk through about the whirlwind I was experiencing and felt that I could trust them. It felt like

I was having a total breakdown. I couldn't think straight, I couldn't eat, I couldn't concentrate and all I wanted to do was die. My brain and my emotions were on overload. These women suggested that I go to a psychiatric hospital for help immediately. I trusted them and took their advice. By the end of that day, I was checked in as a patient.

I had no idea what had been happening to me. It was like I was on the scariest roller coaster and I was crashing at the bottom. My intake nurse asked me if I had been taking any medication. I told them about the Prednisone. She asked if I'd been taking it regularly and I said no, because I hadn't been sleeping regularly. I took it when I could. She told me that this information explained a lot. I was experiencing bipolar symptoms of manic depression as a result of this powerful steroid.

The next morning, I assumed I would be free to leave since we determined that I wasn't crazy or having a nervous breakdown. I was wrong. Since I had checked myself in and signed the forms, I had to stay and be monitored and evaluated for a week. They wanted me to detox from the medication and protect me from harming myself. I was trapped.

The place was cold and stoic. The walls were made of white concrete and the mirrors consisted of fake glass. It felt like an institution. Nothing inside the building would allow a patient to cut herself. Meals were always on time and there was a rigorous schedule of therapy meetings. As clarity started to return to my brain, I could hardly believe where I was. My life had come to this.

Over the next few days, I settled into the routine of the therapy sessions. Many stories were worse than mine by miles. Not only did hearing their stories help me to feel like I wasn't alone, but they also made me realize that things could have been a lot worse for me. There was a sense of belonging that was established in the meetings, where patients opened up about their own lives, so I felt comfortable enough to start to share about the rape. Talking to a group of people about it was very different than talking to a therapist. It was allowing me to release some of the memories and feelings that had come to the surface during my manic episode.

The week went by very slowly, but it was good to have opened up to others about what I had been through. Seven days did not change my life per se, but it did give me perspective and outlook for my future. I did not want to cycle down a rabbit hole of destruction, yet wanted a full life, one where my hopes and dreams came to pass. I desperately wanted to be whole again. Emotionally complete and not broken.

After seeing the lives of the other people at the facility and digging deep into my own issues during those few days, I realized how bad my life could get. I didn't want that kind of life for myself. I wanted to live life to the fullest and go after my goals and dreams. I didn't want my past to hold me back from my future. Being in a psychiatric hospital for a week lit a fire in my belly. Those few weeks of mania brought the issues of my rape up to the surface and I had begun to dive full force into artistic expression in order to cope. As terrible as the event was, it became a springboard that propelled me into the next place in my life.

Once I was released, I pressed on with the stoic counselor and my artistic expression through writing and painting. Art seemed like it might be a means of healing, so I continued on an artistic path of writing and picked up painting. It was around this time that I discovered I could act.

The summer between my junior and senior years of high school, I auditioned for a local play. I was cast and ended up receiving rave reviews of my performance. This filled me in a way I hadn't felt since I was a figure skater. It was a welcome relief from the turmoil of the previous years. I realized I could dive into a role and become someone else, using thoughts and emotions from my own personal experiences. It was a way of expressing myself without having to be myself.

One step led to another when a cast member in the play had told me about our local university's film department, who cast locals in their projects. Rising out of the fog of the past several years was the bold Simone of her childhood. I marched down to the film department, filled out paperwork and began to audition. To my surprise, I started to get cast for several roles in different student films.

Acting was a new bright spot in my life and I was loving every minute of it. I started to feel alive in a way that I hadn't since I was a kid. A new dream and hope were birthed within me.

Although my acting was going great, my life was still set against the backdrop of my small hometown. In it was a cast of characters who seemed to know all about my past and promiscuous behavior. It felt like the demons that had chased me for years lurked around every corner. I longed to get out of town for good.

In the Fall of 1993, when I was nineteen, I visited San Francisco on vacation with my parents and fell in love with the city. It embodied a sense of acceptance for who people are in spite of their past and present. I desperately needed that in my life. In fact, in many respects, the artistic culture encouraged turning emotional pain into art. That excited me because I desperately wanted something good to come of the trauma I had endured. I started to see that my creativity was a way to express myself and make a connection with others through performing.

A few months after the vacation with my folks, after the stint in the psychiatric hospital, I packed up my bags and hopped on a plane to California. No job, no housing, just the clothes on my back. My parents agreed to cover my expenses for a month and then I was on my own.

I quickly found my stride in San Francisco, just like that little girl who hopped on a Swiss tram and rode into the city to purchase that Tears for Fears cassette tape back in 1985. Here was the "old Simone" who was motivated for something and went after it. I'd had enough of letting my past hold me down and a newfound drive was birthed in me. Within one month, I was hired for three different jobs and moved in to a studio apartment on Nob Hill, one of the most exclusive areas in San Francisco. It was then that my life took another turn.

I worked at a café in the financial district of San Francisco and one morning, a made for television movie was shooting outside our door. The crew members came in and out buying coffee and sandwiches all day long. The idea of Hollywood always fascinated me and of course, when I was a little girl, I'd dreamed of being on the big screen. Suddenly, there it was, right in front of me.

One of the members of the production mentioned that they were looking for local extras for the show. I said, "I'll do it! Where do I sign up?" He gave me the name and contact of a casting director. In true Simone fashion, I got myself cleaned up the next day, went down to the casting office, signed up and had a Polaroid photo taken. Within a few weeks, I was doing extra work on movies and tv shows shooting in the Bay Area.

At that time, I didn't have a car, so I would hop on the local transit to get to every set I was booked on. It was apparent that my zest for life was returning, and my childhood dreams seemed to be in reach again.

I was determined to make something of the opportunity for a film and tv acting career. I sought out a local headshot photographer to get the ball rolling. As I was getting my black and white headshots retouched at a photo lab (before Photoshop was invented and it was done manually), the guy working on my picture told me about an acting coach. I called the coach that day and was soon in an on-camera acting class once a week.

It was in this class that I started to learn what film acting was all about. I attended 2 days a week with a cast of other characters. It was here that I could really explore my talent. We worked on scene study, commercials, and improvisation. When I walked out of every class, I felt alive and purposeful in a way that I hadn't since I was skating.

My acting coach taught me everything that I needed to know about the business. It was still the 90's and nothing had gone digital yet, so we worked with paper headshots and resumes, which we stuck into large envelopes to send to agents and casting directors. He taught me "who's who" of the local San Francisco scene and with some legwork, I got my first interview with one of the top talent agents in the city.

I prepared my monologue in preparation, worked with my coach on how to answer questions that might be asked, and carefully chose a fitted black dress for the interview.

The agent's office was in a historic high-rise building downtown. My nerves were palpable. I walked in, took a historic, but rickety elevator up to his floor and walked into the office. The waiting room was filled with stacks of headshots, books, plays, and photos of actors on the walls. It was like I was in New York City, just off-Broadway, and meeting with a high-powered agent. The surroundings inspired me. It was as if my future lay in this office.

The agent came out of his office, reminding me of a Jack Kerouac or Sam Shepherd. I could tell that he was creative and loved the arts, but he also had an air of self-importance. He came out to greet me, we exchanged a few laughs, which broke the ice, then I auditioned for him.

When I was finished, we chatted for a while and he gave me some good news. He told me that he thought I was extremely talented. He also gave me some bad news: that he didn't have any roles for a plus sized model, so he would pass on me being added to the roster.

The wind was knocked out of me. Sure, I carried an extra 30 pounds on my 5'6" frame, but didn't he just say I had talent? Didn't that count for something? I sat there high above busy Market Street listening to the clanging of trolley cars in the distance and trying to digest the information.

In 1994, a plus size model or actress wasn't as accepted in society as is the case today. Those were the days of the Ally McBeal tv series, and Calista Flockhart looked like she was going to blow away with the next strong wind. I grew up surrounded by a culture that celebrated "thin", in my home with my parents and my sisters, in my high school, on television, in film and in magazines and that carried into the 90's.

My confidence leaked out like a helium balloon with a puncture. Regardless of what exactly he had said or how he had said it, my ears heard the words, and my brain perceived that he was saying I was fat and ugly. This apparently determined whether or not I was good enough to be a film or television actor. There were those lies again: I am not good enough and I'm fat.

The meeting with the agent tipped me over the edge. I felt rejected. I was disgusted that my body would keep me from being a successful actor. I was mad at myself for being overweight. I was embarrassed and ashamed.

Just as I was getting a secure footing in this new city and my life as a whole, it was as if I lost my balance and was spiraling down. The momentum that I had going in my newfound life came to a screeching halt. I felt so low and hopeless that I began to have thoughts of killing myself again.

There were nights when I plotted my walking route to the Golden Gate Bridge to hurl myself over. I only lived about a mile away. I'd think of how for a moment I would be free falling and then nothing. But these thoughts also scared me. I was in a constant limbo of not wanting to go on living and yet holding on by a thread. Like walking a fine line between death and life.

I needed to get away. The walls of my life felt like they were closing in on me and even though I lived in one of the most beautiful cities in the world, my surroundings did not help the claustrophobia I was experiencing.

Somewhere along the way, I decided that no, I wasn't going to jump off the Golden Gate. I was going to fight. I can't explain where it came from, but it bubbled up from inside me. There was a thin shred of hope in my being that breathed strength into my life. Something fresh and new had been birthed in me with the opportunity to be a working actor, but if my weight was the thing standing in the way of this becoming a reality then I was going to do everything in my power to shed it and be thin.

My parents were on another sabbatical in Switzerland. I asked them if I could come visit. I wanted to escape and return from Europe as a completely new person. I was also on a mission to show everyone, including that talent agent, who I really was underneath that layer of fat. I had a newfound reason to hate my body, seeing that it was stopping me at the threshold of living out my dream of being an actress and a model. What happened in that office in San Francisco only fueled the fire for my abuse towards myself.

The trip marked the time when my issues with food and weight turned into a full-blown eating disorder. In simple terms, I wanted to be thin or die trying. I believed that my gateway into working as an actress had to do with my body. If I was skinny, then I could work. That's more or less what that agent had said to me. I thought, "If I can transform my body, I can transform my life." But this drive ran deeper than what the agent had said to me during my audition.

I had allowed myself to be sexually abused for years at this point of my life. A fight rose up within me. The fierce determination to lose the weight was, at the core, about shedding my flesh and the heavy weight of my past in an effort to become a new person. I remember looking at myself in the mirror countless times over the course of those years saying, "I hate you." I was disgusted by my flesh. It wasn't beautiful to me and had not served me well. As far as I was concerned, my body was the reason I had been raped and now it was keeping me from the one passion I found after all the years of depression: acting. I had no regard for my flesh, because it had betrayed me, so I would beat it into submission.

I moved to Switzerland with a laser-like focus to lose the weight. I starved myself, only eating vegetables for months. I exercised obsessively with several hour-long sessions twice a day. I didn't care if I harmed myself in the process. A warrior rose up in me when that agent told me, "no", and I was now in a battle with my past and was willing to die for the victory. Every pound of extra body weight that I shed embodied the emotional heaviness that had never been dealt with. What was, in reality, only thirty extra pounds on my five-foot-six frame, felt like two hundred pounds to me. It felt like my skin was crawling, and I wanted to get as much of the old Simone off of me as I could, desperate for a fresh start.

My parents were impressed with my determination. Most people watch with admiration as someone works hard to lose thirty pounds. As I started to lose the weight, I also got compliments from their friends. Nobody realized the significance of what I was trying to do, what I was trying to accomplish through this weight loss, least of all me. It wasn't until years later, and even during the writing of this book, that I made the connection between how much I hated my body as a result of being raped. We all thought that I simply wanted to lose weight, but it was a deeply emotional experience.

All of it and more came off within a few months. I was lighter and smaller than I had ever been. Even as a figure skater some six years earlier, I'd not been so thin. My ribs were showing. I'd put my legs together and nothing would touch. None of my old clothes fit, and for me, that was a triumphant place of victory. I felt like a new woman. I thought I had achieved victory.

Within a few short weeks of returning to San Francisco, I marched into that agent's office unannounced and said, "Do you remember me?" He didn't. When I told him who I was he was floored, impressed with my determination and wowed by my new figure. He signed me on the spot. Within a month, I booked my first commercial for Chevrolet as a Screen Actors Guild actor. I had done it. I was now convinced that my "skinny body" was the link to a life of success in this industry. I believed that I could achieve anything I set my mind to.

I was twenty years old and began to work as an actress and a model on a regular basis. Some days I would make thousands of dollars for a few short hours of work. It was like a whirlwind. Just a year and a half prior, I had been trapped in my small town in Pennsylvania. Then, all of the sudden, I was working for some of the world's largest companies in their ad campaigns: Marlboro, Eddie Bauer, Rite Aid, Chevrolet, Pepsi, Bank of America, AT&T, and countless others. I was also acting in feature films and television shows that were shooting in San Francisco. Some of the biggest names came to town and I got to work alongside of them: Robin Williams, Don Johnson, Martin Short and more.

For the most part, the routine of booking a job and being on sets was the same everywhere I went. A few days before a photo or video shoot, I would be pre-fitted in fabulous clothes (think Hugo Boss and Ralph Lauren), which the stylist would pin so that he or she could tailor my wardrobe for me.

I would then show up on the day of my booking, at my call time, which was typically at an ungodly hour like 5:00 a.m. That meant waking up at 2 or 3 in the morning. just to be showered and have enough time to arrive, park and find out where I needed to go. Then I would go to get my hair and face done in a trailer where I would be completely pampered and made to feel beautiful.

I'd go back to the wardrobe and slip into my clothes which should now fit like a glove since the tailoring had been finished (secretly hoping all the while that I hadn't gained any weight in the two days since my fitting). After this, I'd head to set to be either the star of the scene or get to work a smaller role with a famous actor for a few days. It was like this every time until it became a normal way of life for me, except for the part where I was being made glamorous to go on camera. I would shoot something that would be seen across the country and possibly the whole world.

Acting and modeling was exhilarating. I felt successful because I was accomplishing the dreams of performing that I'd had since I was a child. Oftentimes, I felt like a star, which is hard to describe, but if I were to break it down, I would say I felt beautiful and worthy. It was as if I was finally chosen, finally "liked" and accepted. It was like I was walking in a dream.

I did all of this while attending college full-time. My parents and I agreed that a college degree was something that I had to get. It was a non-negotiable in our family. I was accepted into a University of California school and would juggle classes between driving to auditions and working on sets. It was a busy and fruitful time when I felt like I was walking in my purpose in life and doing what I was born to do. This was the first time since figure skating that I felt such fulfillment.

There was a place deep down inside of my heart that wanted to face my fears and conquer my battles. This took shape on my 21st birthday. Most people celebrate this milestone year with going to the bars and getting as drunk as possible. Since I had done that more times than I could even count in the previous 10 years, I decided to do something that scared me, so that I could conquer one of my biggest fears. It became an outward expression of how I wanted to live my life.

This takes me back to the story, when I was 10 years old and my parents took me to Paris. It has since become my favorite city in the world, but it was also a place that I realized one of my greatest phobias to heights.

Ever since I could remember, my Dad has had claustrophobia in elevators. Wherever he goes in the world, he has to make sure that he is able to take the stairs in buildings and hotels, often calling ahead to ensure they have a stairwell for him to use. This was never more apparent than our visit to the Eiffel Tower.

To get to the top of the historic monument, there is a tiny elevator. That wasn't going to work for my Dad, so he and I started off on the stairs. We only ascended for about 15 minutes when my knees started to shake, got dizzy, and started to have visions of falling through the cracks of the stairs, plummeting down to the ground. There was a point that was so intense for me, that I couldn't go any further. It was one of the most frightening experiences of my life.

Ever since that day, I had an intense fear of heights. It plagued me. But conversely, I was a mountain girl. I loved hiking, of course, but I wanted to take my experience in the mountains to a whole new level.

I attended a university located only a few hours drive from Yosemite. As I was approaching my birthday, I happened to meet a group of rock climbers. They were passionate about the sport. As a woman who had grown into someone who was keen on taking risks and challenges, I decided to sign up for a climbing class over my birthday weekend.

The group of us packed up and drove to Tuolumne Meadows towards the eastern side of the park. I was ready to conquer my fear, as we roped up and began to climb the first wall. At first, I was shaking in my fitted climbing shoes, but once I realized that I was secure on the rope, I started to relax.

We climbed all day the first day, learning skills for hand and foot placement. In many ways, it incorporated the balance that I had developed over the course of my figure skating career. It was like ballet dancing on a rock. Once I got high enough in elevation, I was brave enough to take in the breathtaking view. I started to feel so free and proud of myself for taking the first few steps.

By the second and third day of climbing, I became one of the most advanced climbers in our novice group. It was like something came over me to drive me to the top of that rock. My final climb of the weekend was with one other instructor. It was the most challenging climb that we could conquer in that area and I completed it.

I'll never forget that weekend when I decided to conquer one of my greatest fears. The brave little girl who lived life boldly before she was raped had made a resurgence. It set a precedence in my life from that day forward. I realized that I was able to tackle hard things, even if they made me shake in my boots. And over the course of time, I would slowly, but surely, begin to be molded into that rugged girl who would tackle hard feats.

Chapter 4

Metamorphoses: "a change of physical form, structure, or substance especially by supernatural means"

I wasn't aware of it then, but I look back on this time and realize that I believed that if I could be a successful actress and model, I would trump my past. The best way to describe it is that I wanted to give a big middle finger to the man who raped me, the ones who used me, those who slandered my name, and all the rest who hurt me along the way. I was going to show them what I was capable of and how I could rise like a phoenix out of the ashes of destruction. I had a new sense of confidence in my life, a purpose, and a newfound passion.

During these successful years, I was still in the dark throws of my eating disorder. Now that I was "thin," there was a huge amount of pressure on me to keep myself at this weight. Actors and models are supposed to stay the same so that every time they are submitted on a project then audition for it, their "look" is consistent. If I were to gain even five or ten pounds, my appearance would change. So, I tried to eat as little as possible and exercise as much as I was able. I was up to running ten miles per day on top of auditioning, working, and going to school full time.

The depression was slowly creeping back into my life. I was now like a hamster who was spinning on a wheel, but couldn't get off. The wheel was my eating disorder and I was headed nowhere with it.

I also started to put myself back into promiscuous sexual situations. Given my past, I knew of no other way. I met a guy in college around the time I really started to work a lot on camera. He was on a successful university sports team, he belonged to a fraternity, and he was funny and intelligent. He seemed to be fascinated by the fact that I was a working actress and model. I think for him, part of the reason he was dating me was to show off to his friends that he scored a model. For me, dating him meant I could have some sort of "normal" college life that I never got to have while I was in my hometown growing up. But just like I had become accustomed to, I slept with him almost immediately after we met and it became almost solely about sex. It wasn't at all pleasurable for me, but rather it was all I knew to offer a man, and it was all I knew to receive from one. With a relationship based only on sex, it's no surprise that it fizzled out shortly after it started.

I now call my sexually promiscuous behavior "sexual abuse" because it was self-destructive and dangerous without regard to emotional or physical consequences and repercussions. I still had an abusive mentality toward my body, so I didn't care very much about who I shared it with. As I moved into my twenties, I began to try to achieve a sense of freedom through my actions.

I turned the tables around in my head and tried to think about it from a different perspective. I was having sex because I was personally choosing to do it, rather than have someone force me. I flipped the script with what I believed to be strength. If I made a conscious decision to purposely put myself in a sexual situation, then it meant I was somehow a free and independent woman. It sounds like the cry of feminism and in many regards it was. I was grasping at straws for a sense of strength in this area.

Unfortunately, this was not at all "liberation" for me as I had hoped it would be. It was the continuation of me being chained to a pattern of behavior that was physically dangerous and emotionally unhealthy.

With every sexual encounter, I walked away with a fear of being pregnant or having a sexually transmitted disease, and with an even greater void of emotional emptiness inside of me. That emptiness encompassed a mixture of sadness, loneliness and depression, all lumped together in one big black hole that started to suck me down once again. But the fighter inside me started to arise.

There were a few short relationships with men who respected and treated me well, but then I broke up with them. One of these was a sweet guy who I met at a local San Francisco tea shop. I'd go there several times a day to study and write my papers for my college courses. It's a typically chilly city, so sitting with a pot of tea was perfect for the creative student. He was there about as much as I was and eventually, we started to talk, engaging in long, deep conversations.

He was incredibly intellectual and a poet. I remember that he had the most gentle spirit, like he would never hurt me. I was drawn to that comfort. He also saw me for more than what I was on the outside, which was new. I loved to read, write, discover, look at art, talk about film, and so did he.

We eventually spent time together outside of the tea shop going on long walks. It was strictly platonic, but I sensed that he really liked me more than just a friend. He was handsome, and in many ways, beautiful. After a few months, we went on a drive up the northern California coast together. It was so comfortable, but as much as I wanted to be attracted to him, I wasn't.

I was so accustomed to men wanting me for sex right away that anything different from that scenario just didn't feel normal to me. Like a soap opera, there had been so much drama surrounding my encounters with men. They were almost always sexual and passionate from the beginning, so if it wasn't like that, I was bored and not attracted to the person. That was the case with this man and a few others who came along.

I was so emotionally numb from the years of abuse that I couldn't comprehend something normal: a man actually liking me for my intellect, my personality, and even caring for me as a person. This man did. His kindness was foreign to me and made me feel uncomfortable.

Love and respect was all I desperately wanted and needed, yet when I had it, I pushed it away. I'd just never been attracted to someone who was not a predator. This was another "side effect" from the rape that existed in my life: I wanted to be loved, but I wouldn't allow myself to be.

It was during these first few years of my twenties that I began to realize the impact that the rape was having on my life. I started to have flashbacks of that night when I was fourteen years old, and I started to grieve. But in these periods of intense crying all I knew how to do was continue the cycle of sexual abuse, beating up my body through the eating disorder, and driving for success towards my next goal. Nothing I did masked the pain for long. But that didn't stop me from trying.

Not long after my mini relationship with the poet, I met a model in the same tea shop. But this man was very different. He was tall, dark, handsome, alluring, and sexual. To be admired by such a gorgeous man was intoxicating. He seemed to melt away all my pain and my fears. For a girl who identified herself as unworthy for so long, I felt special. We started dating and got into a relationship with break-neck speed.

It was the first time I really lived out a "romance". Before that time, I can't remember being in much of a relationship. The backdrop for our love was San Francisco. We would go out to dinner, stroll the streets, and sit in cafés together for hours on end. And of course, there was sex. I was passionately in love.

Shortly after we started dating, he left for Italy on a modeling assignment. He was to be gone for several months and I was heartsick. I had become a go-getter, so having been to Europe several times before, I knew how easy it was to buy a ticket to fly there to visit him. I did exactly that. Within a few weeks of him leaving, I was back in his arms again, strolling around another breathtaking city: Milan. It was like my life was straight out of a movie.

I returned back to the states while he stayed overseas for a short time longer, then he returned. He asked me to marry him with a cheap ring he bought in a corner store of Union Square. I said yes and I thought this was it.

The thing about whirlwind romance is that it is deceiving. You fall in love rapidly without knowing the person's true colors. This was the case with us. Once he got a ring on my finger, his controlling nature started to rear its ugly head. What started out as a textbook romance, ended up being a nightmare.

Underneath his gorgeous exterior was a dominating man. Almost instantly after we decided that I would become his wife, he started to treat me horribly. He put me down, bad-mouthed me, and manipulated me. He was full of jealousy and didn't want me to even so much as look at another man. Yet, when I went into the café where we had met, the female employees warned me that he had been in there without me trying to pick up other women.

I'd also kept journals since I was 16 years old, which compiled approximately seven years-worth of writing. They included the kinds of details that I'm writing about in this book. One day, when I was out auditioning, he opened them and read each page. They were my secret, private writings, where I processed my pain on paper. Every word represented the heartache and wrestling for acceptance that I went through over the years.

When I got home that evening, instead of him responding in a loving way, he was angry and used everything he learned against me. He called me a slut. He said he was disgusted by me and he made me throw my journals out. Which I promptly did. I was in love, after all.

It took some time to realize what he was doing. He wanted a woman he could control. None of it felt right and all of the passion I had for him started to slowly disintegrate over the next few months.

I knew that I didn't want to be controlled. I'd already lived through some diverse experiences in my life up until that point and I began to realize that I had a choice to either stay with him or walk away. I didn't want to be treated this way and, although it took me a few more months to figure it out, it occurred to me that this was how the rest of my life would look beside him. The fighter inside of me rose up. In spite of wrestling with the insecurities entrenched in my soul, I knew that I deserved better than how I was being treated.

This man had moved into my apartment, so I told him to move out. Then he threatened me. I can't remember the exact details of the threats, but I did have to call the police and ask how a domestic abuse situation should be handled. Although he hadn't been physically abusive, he had been abusing me emotionally.

He finally moved out and we lost contact, but not without me learning something invaluable from my experience with him. I was able to make a decision to choose which direction I wanted my life to go. Option one was to marry this man who was abusive to me and would most likely be controlling for our entire marriage. The second option was to go on to be free Simone who lives the life she wants to live without someone reiterating in my ear how worthless she is. I did enough beating myself up for my worthlessness on my own.

The fact that he read my most personal journals continued to resonate with me. I was violated and that caused a tough grit to rise up in me. It was something that I didn't even know existed. I was learning that I am a fighter who is worth more than being someone's doormat.

With my fresh wind of confidence, I decided it was time to pack up my belongings, say goodbye to San Francisco and head to Los Angeles to further pursue my acting career.

I moved right after graduating from college. My faithful Dad flew out to help me get settled into a room I rented in a small house in Santa Monica, about 2 miles from the beach.

Once again, it was more bonding time for us, which made me feel special. I've always hungered for that from him, just like when we played football and wrestled when I was a kid. His appearances throughout my life are sweet memories for me. I felt loved.

This was part of my healing process in the aftermath of the rape. Even though it was nearly 10 years afterwards, the love and companionship from my father, treating me like a special daughter made me feel important, valued, and worthy.

I moved out of my parent's house at 17 and moved back in a few different times over the years, but I had always been missing that connection with my Dad. In fact, I don't think our daddy daughter bond had ever been quite the same after I became a teenager.

I had been in so much turmoil during the years after my rape. I'd been distant and cold with them and I'm sure they didn't know how to react to that behavior in me. However, I always craved a father's love. To have him spend the time to drive with me on this trip back out west was his way of showing me that he loved me and cared about me.

When women are sexually assaulted, we can have very twisted views of men as predators, evil, and abusive. We feel shame. However, when the love of a father comes in and causes her to feel valued as a daughter, this can change her life. It did mine.

I started to realize that a man can love me in a pure and holy way. I believe that in these years when my Dad stepped in to help me move, spend time with me, hike with me and dine with me, my broken heart started to fuse together and I took steps forward towards becoming a whole woman. It was quality time that we got to spend together, which brought a lot of mending to my heart after years of feeling abandoned and alone.

My parents were also always so supportive of my acting career. They loved seeing me on the big screen, even if I showed up for only a moment in the smaller roles. This helped me in such a profound way over the years. Their love kept me going during times that I felt so lonely. They knew that I battled with emotions and depression, although I don't think they fully understood why or how to help in the right ways.

Their support of my career was their way of helping me through it and it did. Looking back over my life, I could never have done the things that I did without them. When my Dad showed up to help me move, it was another show of love from them that I desperately needed.

It was an exciting time for me as I settled into Los Angeles. I was 23, I'd been successful in the San Francisco entertainment market and now I was embarking on Hollywood. This was the big time. I felt that my life was "somehow" lining up just for this moment in preparation for me to live in one of the largest cities in the world and work as an actor.

The start of my career in LA did not begin with a bang. I had no idea what I was doing or how to go about getting in the door to start to audition for film and television. I'd been a "big fish" in a "small pond" in San Francisco and now it looked like I might be a flop. After years of working there, all the top casting directors knew me, but in Los Angeles, I had to start from scratch.

Back then, all submissions for projects were done with paper headshots. The internet was yet to be in full swing. Nobody knew me in Los Angeles, so I had to introduce myself one by one. I started mailing out hundreds of black and white headshots with resumes stapled to the backs. It was a daunting task to break into the market.

In the meantime, I travelled up to San Francisco to audition and work jobs on a regular basis. It kept me moving and productive in front of the camera and it kept me motivated to press on in LA, even when no responses came back from my mailings to agents and casting directors.

I put on a brave face as I continued on with my acting and modeling career, but behind closed doors, I fought with my eating disorder more intensely than I ever had. Living in Los Angeles will wreak havoc on anyone with a distorted self-image and low self-worth. The city constantly bombards its inhabitants with images on billboards and people walking down the street who look gorgeous and perfect. It made me feel like I wasn't good enough to fit into that corner of the world.

There were times when I watched a commercial or saw a print ad and thought I looked "thin enough". There were others that made me angry at myself for letting my body gain weight. My eyes always went to scan my body size and shape with harsh criticism. My mind played tricks on me, so I combatted them by exercising harder and eating less.

Within a year, I was 24 years old and found myself living with a boyfriend, who I will call "Don", in a chic Los Angeles neighborhood called Los Feliz, right next to the heart of Hollywood. The apartment in

Santa Monica was sold by the landlords, so I was forced to move out suddenly. Don asked me to move in with him, so I did.

He was successful, had money, owned a house, was educated and intelligent, kind, loving towards me and we had a lot of fun together. It was a comfortable life, one that I needed after moving to such a sprawling and intimidating city. We had two dogs, a group of friends, a big backyard where we would eat organic meals and drank Bloody Marys. We also loved to travel.

We lived life on a whim, because we could. One night, we were sitting in a restaurant in the Hollywood Hills and started talking about Las Vegas. He asked, "Do you want to go tonight?" I screamed, "Yes!" Within two hours, we were at the Burbank airport, tickets in our hands with adventure waiting for us. This was my life.

My career had also started to move forward in LA with some commercials and print ads. Don supported me financially, so it gave me the time and space that I needed to continue connecting and networking with people in Hollywood.

From the outside, my life was becoming everything that I had dreamed it would be. I lived in a beautiful house, had a boyfriend who loved me, and a blossoming career. Everything was falling into place yet again, but when I woke up every morning, there was a pit in my stomach. I felt empty inside and in the same emotional lockdown I had been in before. I had everything I thought that I had wanted, but it didn't satisfy me.

The most difficult part to wrap my mind around was that, if I stepped out of my body and observed my life, it looked great. But I was trapped on the inside, continually battling with depression and obsession with my weight. I almost always felt less than "enough" on the inside. I don't even know what my gauge for "enough" was, but what I did know was that there was a deep lack of fulfillment in my life and I could not figure out why.

I took the fight out on myself. One day while I was living with Don, I barely squeezed into a pair of size 2 jeans for an audition. Disgusted, I walked into the bathroom and lifted up my shirt to look at my waist in the mirror. Fat was spilling over the sides of the jeans and it made my shirt look lumpy. I stared at my naked belly in the mirror with shame. I grabbed my tape measure and promptly measured to make sure it was still 25". It wasn't. I pinched the inch of excess flesh and said to myself with self-loathing and hatred, "You're fat." It was like I was the pretty, skinny and popular girl in high school attacking the overweight, lonely outsider. Except, these two girls were stuck inside my head, battling it out for victory.

The other issue was my relationship. Don was yet another man who I cared about, possibly even loved, but was not attracted to. I fought this issue really hard this time around, because life with him was so good. We had so much fun together and for the first time in a long time, if ever, I felt like I could truly be myself with him.

This relationship was my first adult relationship in which I knew that he authentically loved me for me and not for what I could offer him sexually. In fact, I didn't feel like a sex object at all with him. He was a genuine man who wanted the best for me. But in contrast, I was like a cold fish when it came to intimacy with him. As had happened before, when a man came into my life who loved me in a pure way, I didn't feel sexual or passionate love for him. I waited and waited until the feelings grew, but in the end, they never did.

I stayed with Don longer than I should have, because I craved the stability and the security that he offered me. To some extent I did love him, but I also used him. In the chaos of my internal battle, I clung to someone, anything that would make me feel solid. It was nice to be loved. At the same time, I was disgusted with myself for living and sleeping with a man that I wasn't attracted to. It was just wrong and I knew it.

The more uncomfortable I was being in a relationship with him, the more I felt claustrophobic, trapped within my mind, emotions, body, and my surroundings. I couldn't continue to live inside the relationship with Don. Depressed and restless, I was grasping at anything to bring change to my life. As hard as it was to leave the comfort and security of my life with him, I decided to move out. I had to move on.

During the next year, I stepped back onto the path of self-discovery. I had to make a conscious effort to do something, anything to change my well-being. I was exhausted from feeling blue and sick and tired of hating my own body. After ending my relationship with Don, I moved to the mountains just outside Malibu. I've been a mountain girl for as long as I could remember, so you can imagine that I believed that moving to this house might be good for my restless soul.

I began to look into self-help books and various books on spirituality. I read about Buddhism and Taoism, about yoga and meditation. They seemed to lay out some solid life principles for me, but they fell short of getting me through my issues. Whatever practices I learned from these teachings only gave me temporary solace.

The problem I found with new age thought was that they always pointed towards finding the peace within myself. How could I find "inner peace" when there was such turmoil? Peace might be somewhere outside of me, like in the mountains or by the sea, but it certainly wasn't in me while the recurring battle of war was raging. I certainly tried everything I could in my own power to find the quiet happiness I so longed for, but nothing seemed to stick.

The principles, teachings, and meditations I was learning from these books weren't bringing me healing or changing my behavior, so I knew I would have to find something outside of myself to radically change me. The next few years would lay the foundation for me to discover that "something" that I desperately needed.

My new home was nestled amongst the trees and my bedroom looked out onto a small pond. At night, I could hear the water frogs chirping in unison. There was a walkway that twisted and turned up a hill opening up to a wooden deck that overlooked the mountains of Malibu. I'd walk up there, sit down, breathe in the fresh eucalyptus scent coming from the trees and read my self-help books about "enlightenment" while journaling my thoughts and feelings. Even as I write this, it sounds like it should have been amazing, but it wasn't.

The problem was, I was desperately lonely, as in dry as a desert desperate. I had a massive pit at the bottom of my stomach. As intensely as I tried to escape every dark feeling and aching sadness I experienced, it was always there, lurking in the mountain tops and in the valleys.

Eventually, the walls of this little house in the mountains started to close in on me and once again, that familiar feeling of claustrophobia came back to haunt me. I felt trapped and isolated. This time, it was more like, when I got alone and quiet with myself, I realized that I actually couldn't stand who I was. All that quiet forced me to start looking at things about myself that I didn't want to face: the rape, the eating disorder, the promiscuity, the drinking. I felt dirty and I desperately wanted to be clean and whole.

My mountain life was also wrought with a landlord who turned out to be a cokehead who edited pornography overnight. Cliché for a Los Angeles story, but also very true. Dealing with him was rocky and tumultuous to say the least. He made what should be a relaxing getaway into a nightmare. I felt unsafe with his erratic behavior. He was claiming that my roommates and I owed him an exorbitant amount for the utilities and threatened to take us to court to pay them.

Beyond that, I was still not able to change what was happening inside of me. Simultaneously, I wanted to "face my demons" and "run from them" all-together. Even though I had fleeting moments of feeling at peace while sitting on that beautiful deck, reading and writing while overlooking that valley, it never lasted. It was only a couple of hours later that I ended up feeling the same way hours afterwards: depressed and hopeless.

An opportunity was presented to me to move to Venice Beach, so I jumped on it. I would live only two blocks from the famed bike way that runs from Malibu to Huntington Beach. I was certain that long runs on the sand and fresh salt air would certainly clear my head and settle my emotions. I remember thinking, "It's just what I need!" So, I went from a house in the mountains to a bungalow next to the Pacific Ocean. Even as I write this now, I'm thinking, "That sounds freaking amazing!" But it wasn't.

No matter how much I changed my scenery, where I lay my head at night or woke up in the morning, at altitude or at sea level, nothing was alleviating the turmoil going on inside of my soul. Wherever I moved to, whoever I moved in with, wherever I was, I still wrestled with the same demons. At that point in my life, I actually hated myself. I was also going on five years battling with an eating disorder.

From everything I have learned about eating disorders, once a person is entrenched in it, it becomes more and more difficult to maintain. Like a drug addict who needs more drugs for a stronger "fix", an anorexic and bulimic needs to employ more drastic measures to keep his or her weight down and to "feel thin". That was me. Starve myself as long as I could, then hit the boardwalk and run as fast and as hard as I could for as long as I could. Burn that fat and stay thin. That was my mission.

When living at the beach didn't change me, I was completely done with Los Angeles. My acting career was only just puttering along after almost two years of living there, so I took a long hard look at my life and asked myself, "What do you really want to do?"

I wanted to radically change my life yet again. But this time it was different. The longer I stayed depressed, the more I just wanted my life to end, but I couldn't. I still had fight left in me. And even though I kept bouncing from location to location seeking inner peace, at least I was trying. I wanted to change.

The endurance to keep on keeping on was growing in me. I wasn't going to be satisfied with where I was, with a life of sadness and self-loathing. So, I did what I knew how to do: move on. I packed up everything I owned that would fit into boxes, shipped it back to my parents' house in Pennsylvania, and flew back to Switzerland.

I stayed with my parents' friends in Zurich for two months. This is where I had gone early on in my acting career after the episode with the talent agent who told me I was "plus sized". Europe had always felt like an escape from reality for me. It was like being back in my childhood; A time when I was bold and creative, taking the tram through Basel, painting pictures of churches and wanting to be a fashion designer.

There was something about being in Switzerland this time around that gave me real hope for my future.

Much of my days were spent roaming the streets, riding the trams I loved so much, drinking coffee, smoking cigarettes on café patios, taking in the medieval architecture, soaking up the language, eating Swiss delicacies, and ending my days with a glass (or four) of wine on the veranda talking with my mom's friend. We spent hours talking about what was going on with me and I was able to process some of what I had been feeling and experiencing with her.

These months at age 25 proved fruitful for clearing my head. I had a lot of time to think through what had worked and what had not worked in my life. I planned for the next move.

Being away from the entertainment industry for the first time in 5 years gave me a fresh perspective. I was tired of the superficial fixation of beauty in Hollywood. It was compounding my internal struggle with self-hatred. I desperately wanted to escape the "standard" of what I was "supposed" to look like and what I thought I should look like. My focus wanted to be on who Simone was inside and her life's purpose.

After lots of thinking and journaling, I was sure that I still wanted to be an actor. Deep in my gut, I felt like my career wasn't over. Since that was the case, I decided that I was going to become the best that I could.

Since high school, I had wanted to get formal acting training. Now that I was in my mid-twenties and the world had entered into the new millennium, I surmised it might be time to go for it. My mom's friend, the one with whom I was processing my next steps with while at her house in Zurich, is from England. She suggested that I apply to drama schools in London since some of the greatest talent on stage and in film come out of the UK.

A spark was lit inside me and my internal drive and excitement came alive again.

It was the year 2000 and the dial-up internet was slow, but I took her suggestion and jumped on the "world-wide-web" to look for schools in London. It turned out that I just happened to be within the application and audition window for schools that started classes in the late summer and early fall, so I needed to act fast.

Almost as soon as I had my applications filled out and mailed them off to the schools, I received my audition dates. They were conveniently scheduled within a two-week window. So, with all the boldness I had within me, I booked a flight to London to audition for some of the most prestigious schools: Royal Academy of Dramatic Arts, London Academy of Music and Dramatic Arts, Central and others. All of them seemed far out of reach for little old me, who had mostly done film work, but I quickly prepared my monologues and set off on an adventure.

I felt way out of my league auditioning at those big schools which produced so many Oscar, Emmy, Tony and BAFTA award-winning actors, but I just went for it. It was like I was using all the pain that I had felt for the last several years as ammunition to propel me forward. With each audition, my nerves rattled as I walked into a huge room with hardwood floors, facing a panel of stoic judges who were taking notes on me and my performance. It reminded me of the movie "Flashdance" when the main character went in for her final audition and danced her heart out. The experience was surreal to me because that particular movie had inspired me to become a performer as a child.

My final audition was at a school established in a large three-story house in West London. When I walked in, I immediately felt at home. I was greeted with a warm welcome which was a stark contrast to all of the larger schools I had just auditioned for in the week prior.

The owners lived on the top level and would come down to teach alongside other staff members. Each "room" was its own classroom, and on the back of the house a theater was added where all of the class performances were held. My nerves transitioned into peace when I got to chat with the head director and found out that he knew my very first agent in San Francisco. It felt like the smallest of worlds in that moment, and I knew it was the right place for me.

I knocked the audition out of the ballpark and was offered a position before I walked out the door that day.

The details of enrolling for the school, finding funding and housing all fell into place like clockwork. Before I knew it, I was moving into a room in a historic house in Ealing, West London. Drama school began in the summer of 2000. My life was beyond exciting during that time. It was there that I sought to, once again, shrug off my old life and move onto the new. I'd found my zest for life again and was pursuing my artistic passions through acting.

The year in drama school did mark the beginning of some life-long changes for me. It was there that I started taking small steps to deal with my eating disorder.

School required a lot of physical energy and I wasn't able to sustain that with the way I had been eating. I'd been starving and binging for years as a result of my obsession with my weight. The schedule of drama school demanded a more healthy, sustainable diet or I wasn't going to complete the work. It was also incredibly reassuring that when it came to acting, the Brits were less focused on appearance and more focused on talent and technique of the craft.

Just before I moved to London, I found a book that taught me the importance of eating balanced nutrition while keeping physically fit. During that year, I committed to consuming a wide variety of foods and working out at the gym five days a week. In fact, I learned how to prepare my characters and learn my lines for my classes and performances in between weight-lifting sets and cardio work. Along with my new class schedule, diet and exercise routine, I also gained a support system from my friends at school.

I never really had a lot of girlfriends while growing up, but friendships were something I always desperately wanted. Figure skating had been a very isolating sport for me, so even though I had some skater friends, I rarely confided in them or felt very close to anyone. After the rape just before my 10th grade year in high school, I felt isolated. Several of the girls that I had been friends with started to talk about me behind my back. After that, I didn't trust most women. In fact, I don't remember having a close girlfriend for the rest of my years in high school.

My friendships during the years following, including college and my acting career, were superficial at best, never going deeper into the experiences and stories of life. This all changed when I rented a room in a house in London at drama school. One of my roommates would become a lifelong friend.

We sat for hours in each other's rooms talking about everything. I was able to talk to her about a lot of painful things that had taken place in my life. I felt safe with her. I trusted that she was not going to harm me further with the information like the girls in high school. It was the first time I was able to process the rape and the sexual abuse with a girlfriend. She not only listened to me, but also accepted and loved me in spite of what she heard.

Being able to open up and confess this was very healing for me. The stories shared in the deep conversations behind closed doors in the rental house with my new friend became an acting tool for me. I would use the memories and feelings that came up in my personal life to channel them into the characters I was preparing for and performing on stage. It became a way for me to process through the pain. I would find deep ways to connect with my characters emotionally, because we had a history of struggle in each one of our lives.

The first character that I prepared for drama school was a mother whose daughter commits suicide while they are living in the same house. As I developed the emotional life of this mother, I discovered that our stories weren't dissimilar. We both struggled with life purpose, depression and we also lost that which was most precious to us: our innocence. She lost her child and I lost my own "child-self" when I was raped. I was able to pour out my loss on stage and process through the dialogue and my character's actions.

Throughout the year, the plays and stories we acted out on stage comforted me. I began to realize that I was not alone in what I had been through, that my feelings and behaviors were part of the human condition. It was my first steps towards healing, to turn something so horrible into something beautiful through my acting.

That one year at the drama program proved very rewarding for me. I was still drinking, heavily at times, but my life overall was becoming more balanced, more focused. I had goals and was feeling purposeful. Towards the end of the year, the small American group of actors got together and organized a showcase off-Broadway in New York. We weren't able to perform in the school's showcase in the West End of London due to visa restrictions, so we took the initiative to organize one for ourselves. We scheduled it for September 10, 2001.

Chapter 5

Attack: "a violent or aggressive assault on one's property or character"

The summer of 2001 leading up to the showcase consisted of a lot of preparation. We spent time rehearsing, organizing flights and housing, securing the theater, sending out invitations, and preparing for our performances. It was an exciting time. I was unsure of what my next step in life would be after the showcase, but I was looking forward towards the unknown.

Our show fell smack dab on my twenty-seventh birthday, September 10th, and I hoped that the trip to NYC would reveal a lot to me. This was a time where I was not fixated on my weight or in deep turmoil and pain.

Drama school had done a lot for my healing process and I distinctly remember having a sense of hope. I'd spent a year being accepted by others, especially my new best friend, in a way I had never experienced before. My body was healthier from a more balanced diet; I had more energy and mental focus. And I felt accomplished when I returned to the States, like there was a huge breakthrough in my life. It was a new beginning yet again.

A young woman from my hometown lived in Manhattan and I had arranged to stay with her during that week. New York had always excited me when I was a little girl. I'd only been a few times, but I felt alive with excitement when I visited. The city pulsated with creativity. For a performer or an artist, it was the place to be.

The entertainment industry in NYC was very different than Los Angeles, which was very commercial and more focused on business rather than the art of entertainment. New York City, with Broadway and all of the small live performance theaters, reminded me that acting is an art, and it inspired me to be the best actor at my craft that I could possibly become. It was with this excitement that I felt supercharged in these days leading up to the showcase. The warm late summer days were lingering and hope filled the air.

While I was staying in this apartment in Gramercy Park days before the showcase was set to go up, my friend's roommate decided that she was going to move out. This created a vacant room, so I was asked if I would like to move in. Without hesitation, I said yes! It was New York City and I had always had a secret dream of living there. Suddenly, out of the blue, here was my chance. It seemed as though everything was lining up for me to say yes, so I wrote out my security deposit check on Saturday, September 8. The showcase was to be that Monday on my birthday.

While the apartment details were being arranged, we were knee deep in preparations and rehearsals leading up to our performances. Our guest

71

list was growing by the day and included talent agents, casting directors and producers. The day of the show finally arrived and we had a great turnout.

When I was a child, I dreamed of stepping onto a stage. I had done it so many times starting in my parent's living room, then local plays, then drama school, but when it came down to the buzz and exhilaration of walking onto an Off-Broadway stage to perform, there was nothing like it. It gave me such joy to perform. I'd come to a place where I could clearly channel my life experiences through my characters on stage, so acting became cathartic for me.

While I was performing that Monday in the Signature Theatre on 42nd Street, it felt like I was in an alternate universe. Yes, I was saying the lines and portraying the character in the scene, but I was also in a sort of "déjà vu", the kind I dreamt about playing out, but was living in that moment, in my flesh. It was as if, when I was a little girl, I knew that I would be exactly where I was on that day, September 10, 2001.

In spite of my past and all of the internal turmoil I had wrestled with for years, nearly everything I had hoped for and expected as a little girl had become a reality: acting in commercials, being a model, performing in feature films and television and now, Broadway. I could not have orchestrated my journey into professional acting any better than it was playing out.

After we finished the show that night, we headed into the Village to celebrate our success and, of course, my birthday. We sat on the patio of a lively bar on that warm night, drinking cocktails, laughing, reminiscing about drama school. It was an absolute blast. It felt like a fresh leaf was being turned over in a new city. It was NEW York City after all. I went back to the apartment (which I would now call home) to get some solid rest that night. The next morning was an important one because I had to wake up early and start looking for a job, so I could support myself living in Manhattan.

I got out of bed at about 7 a.m. on Tuesday, September 11, 2001. After one week of being in the city, I had already settled into a morning routine: grabbing coffee at Starbucks, writing in my journal, and then heading across the street to the gym. This day was no different than the others had been over the previous week, warm and summer-like in the city.

Extra coffee in hand, I headed to the gym to start my leg workout and got on the leg extension machine. I mindlessly glanced up at the television to catch a glimpse of the morning news and that's when I saw smoke billowing out of one of the World Trade Center buildings. The gym was located at 3rd Avenue and 23rd Street, so when I made my way to the window, I could see smoke in the distant sky. Everyone started to gather around the television and chat with each other. In that initial hour, we thought that there had been some sort of fire or a bomb had exploded. Nobody knew the seriousness of what was taking place.

I was finishing up my workout with stretching when the second plane hit the other tower. When that happened, we knew it was an attack. I immediately thought Manhattan was the target and we were under siege. I tried calling my roommates, but there was no answer, because the phone lines were jammed. My parents were also desperately trying to call me at the time, but I later found out that they couldn't get through to me either.

To say that I was scared doesn't even describe what I was feeling. It was a paralyzing fear. Suddenly, I felt trapped at the gym with no place to go. My apartment was a couple of blocks away, but nobody was home and I didn't want to go back there only to be alone while this was happening. I also thought that if I went outside to walk anywhere, that I would be unprotected if something else, another plane, a bomb, would land in the city. Rational thoughts do not necessarily occur during an emergency situation like this. Our brains click into "survival mode", so we're thinking of any strategy that might protect us.

It also became very clear to me that I didn't want to die alone, so I stayed at the gym where other people were experiencing the same thoughts and emotions that I was.

As the day unfolded, everything got worse. I finally ventured outside the gym to look up at the sky to see if there were any planes or missiles incoming.

Firetruck and police sirens were engulfing the atmosphere. The thoughts came flooding into my mind and my heart: Was I going to make it through the day? If I die today, what do I have to show for it? What would have been the purpose of my life? Have I done all I wanted to do? Accomplished everything I wanted to accomplish? Do my accomplishments even mean anything? Will I die without ever getting married or having kids? Will I turn to dust? Will I go to heaven? Is there a hell? There were so many thoughts and questions running rampant through my head as I scrambled to find a place with a landline phone. I wanted to, at the very least, make a call to get through to my parents and let them know that I was safe.

Our apartment was located right next to a police supply store. I thought this might be the next best place to be other than a police station, so I walked in and asked the woman behind the counter if I could use her phone to call my parents in Pennsylvania. She said that all lines were jammed with calls being made into and out of the city, so I wouldn't be able to make the call. However, while I was standing there, we started chatting, sharing our thoughts and fears with each other. It was like we were thinking and feeling the same things, asking ourselves the same question, "Will this day be my last?"

As we were talking, policemen came rushing in and out to grab anything they could take down to Ground Zero. They were moving so fast and their need for supplies was so urgent that she didn't even have time to take money from them, only to quickly get a name and station number for an IOU. When I saw the look of terror on these officer's faces, I knew the situation was dire.

After I left the supply store, I walked aimlessly up and down the streets. I still didn't want to go back to the apartment and be alone.

Hundreds of people, bloody and covered in dust and soot, were flooding straight up 3rd Avenue from the south of Manhattan where the towers were on fire. These were the people who escaped out of the World Trade Center and the surrounding buildings and were quickly running north.

The scene was apocalyptic. I can't tell you where I was exactly when the towers came down, but I knew that this day was devastating and that lives would never be the same again. As the news flooded in about the other planes that were hijacked and had gone down in DC and Pennsylvania, the fear spread from this just being an attack on Manhattan to this being an attack on the United States as a whole.

I eventually made it back to my apartment and connected with my roommate. We decided that we needed to do something to help, so we set out on foot to the closest blood bank to donate blood for the victims. I remember the line wrapped around street blocks. The national guard rolled down the streets of Manhattan in tanks, the bridges closed down, the trains stopped, and there were no planes flying overhead. It was like we were living in a foreign land.

I couldn't believe that this was happening, the day after our showcase, the first day of my twenty-seventh year of life. I'd rarely ever been to Manhattan and I thought, out of all of the places in the world I could be right now, what are the chances that I am here today, September 11th, 2001?

Thousands of precious ones lost their lives that day, but I made it through that day alive. It turns out that my best friend's mother had planned to take us to the Windows of the World restaurant at the top of the World Trade Center for my birthday that morning. For some reason, she never followed through. I had been just a few questions, answers, and a subway ride away from losing my life that day.

9/11 changed my life forever. The existential questions that arose in me that day were haunting. What would have happened if I had died that day? What would I have left behind of value? What would have become of me? Would I go to heaven? Would I turn to dust? Had I lived a life of helping others? Did I have loved ones who I had impacted in a positive way?

New York had effectively shut down after the disaster. All of the casting directors and producers who had come to our showcase the day before were distracted. We were unable to reach them for follow-ups and networking and furthermore, our little showcase seemed unimportant compared to what happened the next day. Film, television shows, and commercials were leaving the city for insurance protection. After an experience like 9/11, acting seemed like the least important endeavor for me at the time. I wanted something more out of life, I just didn't know what.

I got a job selling gym memberships in the city. It was a steady gig, but I was working full-time to pay rent and bills. This left no time for me to get myself out into the acting community, meet casting directors and audition. I also started to have symptoms of Post-Traumatic Stress Disorder (PTSD). Every time I heard a siren, I started to panic. I had anxiety attacks. There were regular bomb and anthrax threats on the subway, so I walked everywhere. I lived in constant fear that more attacks were coming and I was constantly in fear for my safety. The truth was that, for the first time in my life, I was afraid of dying because of all the unanswered questions that had surfaced.

I had become accustomed to having goals and plans for where I wanted to go, where I wanted to be, and what I wanted to do, but just like the thick cloud of smoke and dust surrounded Manhattan after the towers came crashing down, the direction in my life was foggy once again. In the midst of it all, a passion was birthed inside my heart to make a change in my life, stop living only for myself, and start helping others. I longed to walk out deep purpose in my life, but I didn't know where to start.

After several months of trying to establish a solid footing in Manhattan, I decided to move back to my hometown. Although it was the very place I had been raped nearly 15 years prior, most of the people who knew my secrets as a teenager had long since forgotten or moved away.

It was nestled in a quiet valley in central Pennsylvania and I sensed it would bring some clarity, peace, and relief. The comfort of my parent's house seemed like the place to recharge and I needed a slower pace of life to decompress from the tension of PTSD. It was also becoming apparent that I could no longer change my heart, my mind, my emotions, and my thought-life by changing my location, so I had to settle in to one place and battle it out until I found peace.

While the diversity of my endeavors and travels throughout my life were exciting, my escapism had become a pattern. With each radical decision I made, whether it be to move to LA, London, or New York, I hoped that I would find happiness. Of course, I enjoyed every decision I made in one way or another, but I also hoped that it would change my emotional life, that depression and hopelessness would be gone for good. No matter how far I would move far away from a city or circumstance, I wasn't able to run from my problems. My pain followed me to every zip code and through every professional pursuit, my pain followed me. However, I was slowly learning how to face it and it was time to conquer my past.

While I was back in my hometown, I got a job as a waitress. I wanted something simple and easy, so that in my time off, I could explore other opportunities for work and decide which direction I wanted my life to go.

It was there that I gained even more ground in the struggle with the eating disorder. I went back to Weight Watchers and learned more about balanced eating with moderation.

Around this time, I developed a swelling in my neck, which looked like an extremely swollen gland. When I went to the doctor, I was diagnosed with hypothyroidism. I later learned it can be caused from extreme dieting. My hormones were so out of whack from starving, binging, and over-exercising for years that my body was fighting itself. The diagnosis also explained some of the depression I had been experiencing over the years. I was put on medication to regulate my thyroid, but in order to be healthy, I would need to learn how to eat a balanced diet. If I didn't, my body would continue to suffer.

It was now 2003 and life was simple in Pennsylvania. My days were the same and there was little variation from my normal small-town routine. A vacancy grew in my heart. For years, I had tried to fill that black hole with anything I could, from drinking, to men, to acting, to moving to different cities, and anything else that would make me feel whole and complete. The purpose of my life was nebulous. I didn't know why I was here, what I was supposed to do or which direction I was to go into, or what the meaning of my life was. This sounds profound, but it was the core of my deepest struggle. It just didn't become apparent to me until after 9/11.

My heart had changed. I wanted more out of my life, to help people, to change others in a positive way. I wanted to do something meaningful with my life, but I had no clue what that would be. Acting seemed like the only avenue for my career. I'd been pursuing it for nearly 10 years, so it was the only thing I knew how to do. There was little on my professional resume. I had a bachelor's degree in Sociology, but I couldn't see myself going back to a "normal" life with a nine-to-five job after spending a third of my life being in front of the camera and on-stage.

There was a glimmer of hope when I decided to apply to universities to go back to school to get a graduate degree in acting. Given my background, I thought I would make a great acting teacher. This would fulfill my desire to "give back" and help other people's lives.

I started the process of applying and auditioning for schools. It was September and I flew back out to my alma mater in California to interview for a position in their drama program. While I was walking across the campus that day, I stopped to look up into the sky and randomly, out of the blue, said to nobody in particular, "If there is a God, show yourself to me."

I had come to the end of the rope with Simone and my life. I was constantly searching for purpose everywhere I turned, but I found nothing I was searching for. My last resort was this quick little prayer that meant nothing to me at the time. It was a shot in the dark. I continued on with my drama school interviews and auditions and returned back to Pennsylvania.

Chapter 6

Saved: "preserved; rescued from harm"

One night, about a week after arriving back home from interviewing for the MFA program, I was waitressing at a local steakhouse when a couple came in to dine with their friend. As with most restaurants, guests are sat in rotation among all of the servers, so it was my turn to be sat. They were seated at a table in my section. It's funny how seemingly ordinary moments or encounters can change a life forever, but mine did that day.

These three people seemed to be radiating from their faces, and joy lit up their countenance when they smiled and talked to me. As we started to interact and get to know each other, it was easy to see that whatever they had going for them was exactly what I wanted. They had a peace about life, a solidity, a sense of security and of love that I had been desperately longing for.

They asked me about my life and my background. I instantly felt that I could trust them enough to share that I was going through a really difficult time. Standing there in my polyester outfit littered with boomerang pins and my serving apron wrapped around my waist, I was vulnerable and transparent.

They asked me if I wanted to meet some new people at a church gathering they were having at their house the following evening. I said yes, hopeful that anything would break the funk I was stuck in. At the end of the dinner at the restaurant, they gave me a nice, big, fat tip, which shocked me, because I had come to believe that Christians were cheap and only left paper gospel tracts as tips. (I implore you, my readers, to bless your servers, not only through kind words, but through the dollars in your wallet; it means more than you will ever realize!)

When I arrived at their house the next night, I noticed that everyone I met seemed to have the same joy and peace that embodied the couple who had invited me. It was like they were aliens from another planet, not in a scary way, but in a warm, inviting manner. How could people be so nice and seem so genuinely interested in me? We had dinner, talked and then moved into a time of worship and ministry. I had no idea what those two words even meant.

As I mentioned previously, I hadn't been raised in a Christian family. My parents are agnostic, which is the belief that there may or may not be a God, but that it hasn't been scientifically proven yet one way or the other. I naturally adopted this belief, as children most often do from their parents, but it did leave a door open for me to seek my own faith.

Before and after 9/11, I had sought the deeper meaning of life from Taoism to Buddhism to Tarot card readers, to making up my own ideas of who God was. I found nothing that changed my life or my behavior, yet I always knew that there was something missing in my understanding of life, there had to be more.

In the years leading up to this ministry night, the questions I was asking about my life had become even more pronounced. There was a deep cry of my heart for understanding what my purpose here on earth is. That led me to saying that short prayer on the college campus only a few weeks earlier.

I couldn't comprehend the vastness of this world, this universe, and everything that is in it without thinking that there was something or someone greater out there. As for knowing and understanding the Christian faith, I believed what most people I knew believed, that they are hypocrites filled with hate and judgment. However, it was that night at this couple's house that I was taken aback by the kindness of this group, these believers in Jesus Christ. They were shattering my preconceived notions of what Christians were all about.

Although I felt accepted by this group, I felt very out of place once worship and ministry started. Everyone was raising their hands and had a look of love on their face. In contrast, my face had a look of confusion. Why was I even here, I wondered? I didn't know Jesus, I didn't understand the gospel and I didn't really care to. It didn't seem to me like it was the answer I was looking for.

Eventually, after a few tambourine-led songs and some pronouncement of scripture, I walked right up to the host and told her I had to leave. She asked one question before I walked out the door,

"Where are you at with God?" I said that I didn't know and promptly left.

I got a call from her the next day asking if I would like to go to church with them on Sunday morning. She seemed so kind and genuine in following up with me, so I thought I'd make another attempt to spend time with them.

The church service was great. A pastor from New York City had traveled down to our town to share his testimony of being saved out of gang life and drugs and turning to follow Jesus. It felt like I was surrounded by a great group of people. Afterwards this couple again asked if I wanted to come over to their house again to talk and pray. I said I would.

When I arrived at their home, I was greeted by them along with their friend who had dined with me at the restaurant. He was visiting from another state. We made small talk and then they asked me where I was with God, where I was in life, how I was feeling. Once again, I felt safe with them and opened up honestly, sharing that I was depressed and lost, with tears running down my face. Then they started to pray for me.

As they prayed, I began to feel a peace inside me like I had never known. My belly felt like it had a balloon inside of it that was lifting me up. All of my emotional pain seemed as though it was slipping away. While this man, this friend of the couple, from out of state was praying for me, He said that the Lord was showing him many things about me.

He talked specifically about the time in my childhood when I was rejected and sexually assaulted. He told me that the Lord said He had been there with me and in the times following when I hated myself, when I starved myself, when I had thoughts of suicide and depression. He said He was releasing me of all guilt and shame. The Lord wanted me to know that He was there at every turn, that He accepted me, that He created me in my mother's womb, that He has a purpose for my life. He said the Lord showed him that I'd been seeking purpose for my life, that I had been asking why I had to go through all the pain. All of this was spot on accurate.

He also said that the Lord was showing him that over the previous months, I had been voraciously reading books about kings and queens and their monarchies, because God was preparing my heart to enter the true Kingdom of God. He was right! I'd been staying up until the wee hours of the morning reading book after book about Henry VIII, Anne Boleyn and the history of the English monarchy. It had been a fascination of mine that nobody knew. I read with hunger. Every detail of this man's prayer, every word that he spoke of what the Lord was showing him, was accurate. This is prophecy and it's completely biblical.

You know that feeling when you know that you know that something is real? I suddenly just knew. I felt it deep within my bones that God was real, that He was speaking, that He had been with me all of my life, walked with me through all of the turmoil and pain I had gone through, and that He wanted to bring me through to the other side healthy and whole. The peace and relaxation that I felt was beyond what I could have ever hoped for.

I was encountering Jesus. The presence of Holy Spirit was touching me as my body tingled with chills from head to toe. A feeling of lightness of being and joy was flooding my insides. No substance, no relationship, no exotic destination, no modeling or acting job had ever brought me this feeling, this sensation, this hunger being fulfilled. I was in tears, knowing that I was loved all along and had been saved from the turmoil. Apostle Paul writes in Galatians, "Beloved ones, let me say emphatically that the gospel entrusted to me was not given to me by any man. No one taught me this revelation, for it was given to me directly by the unveiling of Jesus the Anointed One." (Gal. 1:11-12 TPT) At that point, I still didn't even know the story or the meaning of the gospel, I just believed in Jesus.

The next day, my new friends invited several of their friends to their house where I would be baptized. I still barely knew or understood anything about Christianity, but I was ready to plunge full force into the things of God. I wanted to feel that wonderful peace for the rest of my life. I felt strong and safe knowing that my God was on my side and fighting my battles for me. Not once did I point the finger at Him and ask, "Why did you let all of this happen to me?" I somehow intrinsically understood that, in spite of the pain we have to go through here on earth,

He is there to see us through and waiting for us with open arms every moment of every day. That is where I wanted to be: in His embrace.

I was baptized by water in their bathtub and came up feeling so clean, like all the dirt had washed away. It was truly a fresh start for me, like being born again. Afterwards, the group of guests circled around me and laid hands on me and prayed. Several of them prophesied that the Lord was going to use me in a mighty way in the areas of drama and video, that He had a purpose for the things that I had walked through in the past, and that He was going to use me to help set others free.

While they were praying, a gibberish just burst forth from my lips. I came to learn later on that this was my prayer language, or "tongues." I also had my first prophetic vision that day, in which I was in a huge harvest field at the base of a mountain dancing with Jesus.

I would come to know Jesus and give myself to Him completely. In my heart, I knew He was real, I knew He was the Son, and I knew that He died on the cross for me to have this kind of peace. "For God so loved the world that He gave His only begotten Son, that whoever believes in Him should not perish but have everlasting life." (John 3:16 NKJV) I can't explain how I knew this was the truth after all of those years of not knowing Him or believing in Him. But in the depths of my belly, I had a deep resolve and certainty that the gospel is true. When I felt His presence and His peace, that lifelong hunger was finally satiated. It was enough to keep driving me back for more and all I needed.

I looked back on all the twists and turns that my life took to get me to that place where I could receive Him fully. It was no coincidence that I was in Manhattan on 9/11. All of the incidences before and after that day lined me up to come to Him at just the right place and time.

In the days, weeks, and months to follow, I would go on long walks and Holy Spirit and I would have deep conversations. It sounds a bit crazy, I know, but He was teaching me. I would hear His quiet voice echoing the Scripture, "My sheep hear My voice, and I know them, and they follow me" (John 10:27 NKJV). The words in the Bible supported what was happening to me.

One day, while I was watching birds fly in and out of a tree, I heard Him speak about the birds of the air, how He provides for them in their nests and how He was taking care of me just the same. When I got home and started to read the Word. To my surprise I came across a verse I had never read before. Luke 12:24 NKJV: "Consider the ravens, for they neither sow nor reap, which have neither storehouse nor barn; and God feeds them. Of how much more value are you than the birds?" He was speaking to me through Holy Spirit Who now lived inside of me and through His Word, the Bible.

He would also send me on adventures in obeying His voice when I heard Him speak. The day before Thanksgiving, just a few months after I was saved, He sent me on a mission. I woke up and was in my morning routine of drinking coffee, reading the Bible and journaling. I saw a vision of a gas station convenience store across town, about twenty minutes away. He said, "I want you to go there now." I asked why. He said that there was someone there I was to pray for. I didn't really want to get up out of my cozy pajamas and drive across town, but I also wanted to see what adventure the Lord had waiting for me on the other side of obedience.

As I was driving there, I felt tired but also exhilarated. I parked and went inside. I said, "OK, Lord. Now what?" He said, "Wait." So, I waited. I waited and waited and waited. It probably looked like I was casing the joint and going to rob it. About twenty to thirty minutes passed and I heard Holy Spirit say, "There she is." I saw a woman who had just paid at the register and was walking to her car. I ran up to her and said, "Excuse me, I know this sounds strange, but God sent me here to pray for someone and I believe it's you. Is there anything that I can pray for you about?" She started to tear up and said, "Yes, I just came from the hospital where my father was just diagnosed with spinal meningitis, and we don't know what's going to happen to him."

I knew this was a God-appointed meeting and He sent me here for her. I just started praying. No fancy prayers, just whatever came out of my mouth. Afterwards, she looked filled with tears in her eyes, with hope and peace. She thanked me and told me how much she needed that prayer, that touch from God in that exact moment. The Lord had impacted this woman on that cold Pennsylvania morning, and even though I never saw her again, I believe He made Himself known to her father too.

He would always prove to me that His voice was real because His words came to pass. One afternoon, Holy Spirit told me to go to the toy store in the mall and pray for the woman in a black and white striped shirt. I drove over there, parked, went into the mall and waited on a bench in front of the toy store until I saw a woman fitting the description. She finally walked out of the store and I stopped her and asked her if I could pray for her. She said no. I felt slightly defeated, but I prayed for her anyway.

The woman in the striped shirt at the toy store could have been a coincidence. There are a lot of people who wear black and white striped shirts in this world. However, it was the sum of the details He was sharing with me, my obedience, and the outcomes that pointed to Him. I had never known that a person could hear God's voice, but again, it is Biblical. From Genesis to Revelation, God spoke to His people. The outcome of my obedience wasn't always what I expected, like when the woman at the toy store turning down my offer to pray for her, but I knew that it was Him who sent me. He was training me to hear His voice.

It was the passion of my heart to be obedient, and I had sought to obey the Lord in faith at every word. I was walking in pure, childlike faith. I knew nothing else but that I could hear His voice and converse with Him. At that time, I thought that this just happened with every Christian, and that my walk would be this glorious and easy for all the years to come. I couldn't have been more wrong.

Chapter 7

Tumbling: "falling suddenly and helplessly; sudden downfall, overthrow, or defeat"

I was so tremendously thankful to the Lord for saving me and bringing me to this point. One scripture from Luke 7:47 TPT has become a cornerstone in my life: "She has been forgiven of all her many sins. This is why she has shown Me such extravagant love." I wanted to show Him extravagant love in everything I did. It was the passion of my heart.

My faith wasn't just something I believed in my mind, it had become part of my whole being. And I didn't just believe I was free, I felt free. And for several years, I was.

Nine months after I was saved, I was hired to work for a sexual purity ministry for teenage girls. Yep, you read that right. Often, the very areas we are called to minister are from places where we had the fiercest battle.

The owners of the ministry felt that the testimony of what God had done in my life was too good not to be shared with their audience. This was a clear example of the Lord's work of redemption in my life. I had always wanted something good to come out of the rape, the sexual promiscuity, and the abuse I had suffered. Now, in the short amount of time I'd been a Christian, I was able to see God doing something amazing out of all the garbage of my life. It was a dream come true. I finally had purpose.

For the next two years, I organized large speaking events, traveling to them across the country, sharing my testimony, and ministering to thousands of girls. I delivered the Gospel and explained how the Lord came into my heart, changing me from the inside out.

As I told the story of how He set me free, I also taught the girls biblical strategies to help them avoid what I had experienced. Many girls gave their lives to Jesus, and thousands of lives were changed. Women and girls would come up to me after the events and tell me how much my story impacted them. Many had also experienced sexual assault or molestation, battled eating disorders, fought bullies at school, suffered from cutting themselves, and felt very lonely in their fight for freedom, just like I had. They felt like God wasn't there, until they heard my story. As I shared how He had moved in my life, it gave them hope that He would do the same in theirs and could get to the other side of the pain.

I was fulfilling Jesus' command to "go into all the world, preach openly the wonderful news of the gospel to the entire human race!" (Mark 16:15 TPT). I wasn't exactly preaching to everyone in the world, but it was a start. I ached for purpose for so many years and here I was, walking smack dab in the middle of it. There's nothing like helping others through their pain. It filled me with joy that I had never known. God was truly bringing beauty out of the ashes in my life.

While in full-time ministry, seeing lives radically changing on a daily basis, I started to feel that familiar longing for acting. My life was becoming more clearly focused now that I was walking with Jesus. It seemed as though God was leading me to blend ministry and acting together.

As only He could orchestrate, my bosses at the ministry decided to open a Christian high school and, given my background with both acting and ministry, they offered me a position as the drama teacher. In the year prior, I'd applied to several graduate programs in order to get my degree and then be "qualified" to teach acting. I wasn't accepted into a single program. Turns out, God had other plans. My desire to become a teacher was now becoming a reality.

I suddenly had a full life. I was booking speaking engagements, traveling the country and speaking with the ministry, then teaching drama class during the week. God had shifted my life into high gear after all those years of wondering what my life's purpose was. These years were some of the most rewarding of my whole life, but God had more.

I now heard the voice of Holy Spirit and I felt His guidance. It's like He pulled me in different directions, wherever He wanted me to go, guiding me with what He was saying to me through my spiritual hearing and through reading the scriptures, as well as through other people's prayers and prophetic words for me. All of it lined up with the word that God was directing me back to Hollywood. I also couldn't shake my deep desire to return back to acting in front of the camera. This excited me. I was confident that, as a new creation in Christ, my experience in the entertainment industry would be different from here on out.

After all those years of being aimless, the Lord was now in my life and I felt so filled with purpose. I wanted to carry this new life, joy, and hope back into a career that I enjoyed and see where He took me.

Through hours of prayer, I settled on the decision to return to San Francisco where my professional acting and modeling career started more than 10 years prior. I'd loved working for the ministry, but we all knew that this is where God was leading me. With the full support of my friends and family, I packed up my car, hopped in the driver's seat with my Dad as a passenger yet again, and started the 4-day trek across the United States.

This turned out to be another really special time with my father. It was the first time we had spent alone like this since I had been saved. Since then, I had learned about Father God's heart for His children, how He loves us and always wants His best for us.

After all those years of darkness, I had forgotten what it was like to be somebody's daughter. It made me feel loved, the same kind of love I craved after all of those years of loneliness. It made me feel special, after all those years of unworthiness. It made me feel like a kid again, after all of those years of hiding who I really was after the rape. I needed this trip with my natural father, because it reminded me that I was both God's daughter and my Dad's daughter. That I was loved by them in the same way, even when my earthly Dad couldn't always express it the way he might have wanted. One way he showed his love for me was to support me in all my endeavors, including yet another 3,000-mile trek across the country.

Once I was back in California, I settled into a historic Victorian style flat with a view of the Bay Bridge. It didn't take me long until I was back in the groove. I found a great church with people my age, where I quickly started making friends and getting involved with ministry. I joined a small women's group that met once a week and I started personally organizing groups to go out into the dangerous areas in the city to pray for the drug addicts and the homeless. In addition to all of this, I started teaching everything I knew about the craft of acting in my own acting class to several students in a room at my church.

I also stepped back into my acting career, seemingly right where I left off seven years prior. All I had to do was reconnect with the agency I had worked with for years and within a few months of my return, I was working in print ads and commercials.

It was different this time around with the Lord in my life. I felt purposeful, like God was strategically placing me on each and every set for His reasons. He wanted me to open up and care about the people I was working with, listen to the stories about their lives and share about my journey and my path to Him.

There were several times when I prayed for people on set, specifically make-up artists, since I spent so long in their chair each day. I'd ask them about their lives and they would open up to me. Holy Spirit would give me an encouraging word for her or him and oftentimes have me share my testimony of coming to Christ. My mission was to be used by Him to change other's lives for the better.

My life had completely turned around and I was excited about everything I was involved in. I had an acting career and I was in ministry, just as I had heard from the Lord that I would be. It's often the times when we are doing the best and feeling wonderful that we fall for the unexpected. I was about to learn that it is precisely when we are seeking and following after God that circumstances will be set up just right for us to fall.

It was in the middle of this prosperous time that I got into a long distant relationship with a Christian man. We had started off as friends over the previous few years, but we really started to connect once my life was moving forward in San Francisco. He was also in ministry and wanted to be a filmmaker.

We had much in common and it was so refreshing to be communicating so deeply with a man who knew Jesus. I'd only really known and understood guys who were doing everything that I had done before I was saved, including drinking, sex and more. But with this man, we had talks about Christ, what God was doing in our lives, our dreams and destinies, about scripture, and where He was leading us. It was an exciting time for me, since I was feeling things I hadn't for a very long time.

While we were opening up our hearts to each other, I was slowly falling in love. He brought out a vulnerability in me that was rare. It was the first time I had been this way with a man since becoming a Christian. Another new beginning for me.

Since our relationship was over the phone, we could only speculate that we would feel the same way about each other in person. After a few months of communicating, I was scheduled to travel to see my sister and her family who just so happened to live a few hours from him. We arranged to meet decided I'd stay with him and his family for a few days, so we could finally meet face to face.

Almost instantly when I arrived in his city and we saw each other, it was clear that the same chemistry that we had over the phone did not exist in person. We'd grown so close over the phone, but in person, it was like there was a brick wall in front of us. He wouldn't allow me to get close to him, either emotionally or physically. The problem was, I already had feelings for him.

It was clear that something had changed for me and that an old pattern was broken. For the first time, even though I wasn't physically attracted to him, I had fallen in love with his heart and who he was as a person. After so many years of relying on attraction and passion to fuel my desire for a man (and vice versa), I had finally fallen for someone for who he was inside.

It was all so new for me. Since I saw life through new lenses after I came to Christ, I was able, to a greater extent, see this man as God sees him, with all of his tenderness, gifts, talents and sensibilities. I also adored that he loved Jesus and that was a first. So, for me, this "wall" wasn't an obstacle. I had become a changed woman through my relationship with the Lord and this was a clear example of that transformation.

This lack of attraction didn't change anything for me. The initial transition from the phone to being together in person was awkward, but I just assumed that the barrier between us would eventually break down. I trusted that we would grow together as time went on, as we continued on over the next few days with me meeting his friends, dining out, attending a music concert, and going to church. However, it was like we were trying to fit two pieces of a puzzle together that weren't matched, but because I was in love, I was committed.

On my last day, he nervously sat me down. I knew something in my gut felt wrong about the look on his face, but I braced myself for what was to come. He told me that he didn't feel the same way about me in person as he did over the phone. That I was a great woman, but that I just wasn't a fit for him. Here I was, having fallen in love with this man, sitting in his parents' basement, 2000 miles from home, getting punched in the gut with the fist of rejection. My eyes flooded with tears and I started crying.

Deep down inside me, I knew that it wasn't a fit, but because this was my first relationship, the first time feeling love for a man as a new Christian, I wanted to continue on. Even though I wasn't physically attracted to him, it was the rejection of my love that hurt the most. I had allowed my heart to open up to him over the previous months in a way that I had never done before and now, it was as if he handed my heart back to me and said, "Here, I don't want this."

While I was at his parents' house for the next day, the Niagara Falls of tears poured out from my eyeballs. It hit me way harder than I ever expected. In hindsight, I can see that what was happening was that I was facing yet another rejection in my life, like I had so many times before, as if it had plagued me. It was my first heartbreak as a Christian and I had no clue how to walk through it.

The Bible tells me that I should run to God for His comfort. King David did. Barren Hannah did when she couldn't conceive. Naomi did when she lost her husband and her sons. Jesus did while He was being beaten and crucified. I knew the Word of God. I had studied it and believed the words and stories are true, but my mind was trapped from years of believing the same old lies like, "You're not good enough." The break-up triggered thoughts of unworthiness, that I was "unlovable".

I knew that I was loved by God, but I also wondered why, after giving my heart so fully and completely to Him at my salvation, He would allow my heart to get broken again. I could hardly digest that after giving my life to Jesus, I would have to walk through this pain again. Here I was, an actor who had put herself up for countless auditions and been "rejected" several times over, but when it came to the rejection of a man, old wounds opened up in me that had never been fully healed.

One break-up might sound mild, but it was far more devastating for me. I felt so much pain, as if a reservoir had opened up and all those years of torment came rushing back into my mind. What I was experiencing, like I had so many times before in my life, were the same old thoughts of being unwanted, unloved, and totally rejected. The old lie crept back into my head and my heart, "You're not good enough."

This lie now pulsated in my head with even greater intensity, because I knew Jesus now, but I still hurt in the same ways I had as a teenager. I had thought that when I was saved, I would be freed of the cycle of experiencing this pain, especially from a man. I naively reasoned that, because I dedicated my life to Him, He would protect me from ever getting hurt again.

Now it looked to me as if God had let me down. From my vantage point, I had trusted Him and He'd allowed my heart to get smashed. Teenage Simone and all of her coping mechanisms to deal with pain were about to rear their ugly heads.

As I tried to work through the aftermath of the end of the relationship, I continued with my acting career. A few short months later, I was cast as the lead character in a dynamic short film. After taking a long hiatus from film and television while I was in London and New York, it was such a blessing to be cast in such a strong, character driven on-camera acting role. The woman I portrayed was everything I wanted to be, a strong and tough fighter who doesn't flinch under pressure. I got a glimpse of who I wanted to become through her. The Lord was still working in my life and blessing me with fulfilling the desire of my heart to be an actor.

We had a cast and crew gathering after we completed shooting the project. It was my first "wrap party" as the star of a film. I was feeling awesome. I was feeling important, accomplished, and special. I was feeling like a movie star. It was nice to feel so good during a time of pain that seemed to plague me. A time when I believed I was not good enough.

Food was served and wine was consumed. A lot of wine. In fact, I don't remember leaving the house where the dinner was held, because I blacked out. When I woke up the next morning, I didn't know where I was and I couldn't find my car. I was due on the set of a photo shoot for an AT&T print ad in just a few hours and I had to drive over an hour to get there.

By the grace of God, I found my car parked blocks away. I cleaned myself up and made it to set with just minutes to spare. It was becoming clear that old patterns were emerging in my life again. I was saved by Jesus, but my habits of coping with pain were still the same. I was wrapped up in trying to work through my feelings of rejection, low self-worth and now condemnation that I was behaving like the Simone I never thought I would see again.

After the film was edited and ready, it was premiered at a film festival in New Orleans, so everyone involved with the production flew out for the event. Just seven years prior, I had walked away from acting and Hollywood and now here I was, the star of a film at a premiere. It was a whirlwind experience.

Somehow, through our friendship and relationship, I connected the man I had been dating, the one who recently broke up with me, to the cast and crew of my short film. I seem to recall hoping that we would be linked back together someday, so any opportunity that might arise, I would help orchestrate that reconnection. When he decided to travel to the film festival to be a part of our premiere and celebration, I assumed God was at work.

It's funny how we can put our hands on a situation, manipulate it into our favor and then call it "God's work" in the end. I was only 4 years into my walk with Him, which seemed like a lot at the time, but in hindsight, it was the blink of an eye. I had a lot of growing to do. Over the course of time, I would learn that I could certainly try to work things in my favor, to make something happen that was my own will or "help Him along" with what I thought He was doing, but in the end, He would always have His way. As difficult as things were at times, I clung to the scripture, "And we know that all things work together for good to those

who love God, to those who are called according to His purpose."
(Romans 8:28 NKJV).

When we arrived in New Orleans, we got together as a cast and crew
and my "ex" was part of the celebration. The whole film festival was
exhilarating, yet there was still a wall between him and I. I'd hoped that
him being there, seeing me as the star of the film, in a different light
than he had seen me in his hometown, would make things different. It
wasn't. As much as I tried to focus on everything that was good about
my life in that season, the pain was like a cancer that was gnawing on
my insides.

The night that our film premiered, I met a man who was starring in
another film at the festival. He was dark and handsome, incredibly good
looking, charming, and he was into me. It was exactly what my flesh
needed to deflect from the heartache. Everyone went to the bars after
the shows and started drinking. He sat close to me and was intoxicating.
I drank, danced, laughed and was part of the crowd.

It was like I was back to the old me, caught up in a swirl of
temptation. We danced, laughed, and flirted. I consumed drink after
drink after drink, then ended up in his arms for the night.

Some may read this and think, "What's the big deal?" A woman
meets a man and they sleep together. It happens every day all over the
world. We see it in movies and television shows all the time. It's
society's norm. Maybe our friends are doing it, maybe we're doing it
and we don't feel bad about it. But here's the thing: when you feel dirty

for so long, you know what being pure feels like. When you're finally pure, you know what feeling dirty feels like. I knew the reality of both.

There are viral videos that make their way around on the internet and social media. They are of dogs that were rescued from horrible conditions, dirty, matted, and infected. The uplifting story goes on to share how the pups were rescued, cleaned up, treated and now have a new lease on life. They're so happy you can almost see them smiling as they play fetch with their new owner. I was one of those dogs. Yet I just walked right back into the old conditions I had lived in for so long. A mentor saw clearly what was happening to me during this time and shared a scripture with me that still resonates with me today: "As a dog returns to his own vomit, so a fool repeats his folly." (Proverbs 26:11 NKJV). That was me.

It's ironic that humans often go right back to the places in their lives that cause so much pain. After the rape, I ran towards men, instead of running from them. They caused me pain, but I would run back into their arms in hopes that it would be relieved. It's like a person struggling with obesity who keeps eating or the drug addict who is slowly dying but can't stop taking drugs. I kept choosing this cycle of sin, because it was the only way I knew how to cope.

As it was, all those years before Christ, I ran back to sexual sin. These were familiar ways for me, the only paths of coping I ever knew, to drink alcohol, then give myself over to a man At the bar that night in New Orleans, my heart was hurting in the face of a man who rejected me, so

I wanted to feel accepted and imagine, even if for a few hours, that I was loved and cared for in the arms of another man. It made me feel better, if only for a few moments and at times, made me feel like "enough".

For so long, I believed that sex was all that I was worth. If a man wanted me sexually, then I was worthy, which is also ironic, because the rape made me feel worthless. I chased after my own value and self-worth in giving myself over to him. It was almost always associated with alcohol, just as it had been all those years ago. This pattern was pervasive in my life before Christ and I had thought that it was over. After coming to Jesus, giving my life so fully to Him, feeling free and pure, working for a sexual purity ministry for several years, I thought I was completely free from sexual sin.

That night was the tipping point for me. I was doing what I hated to do. It says in Romans 7:15 (NKJV) "For what I am doing, I do not understand. For what I will to do, that I do not practice; but what I hate, I do." I believed God loved me, but if I had really known this through and through, the blaring question was, why was I turning away from Him? Why was I running back to the old Simone? It was like an out of body experience. I knew what I was supposed to be doing: loving the Lord with all my heart, mind, and soul. But after that night, I struggled to get back to my walk with Him, to the joy I felt at the beginning of my relationship, and the peace that had flooded my heart and lifted me up to the heavens like a balloon.

I hadn't always believed that sex outside of marriage was sin or understand why. Heck, for most of my life, I didn't even believe in sin. Just because the Bible said that something was a sin didn't mean that it was "my truth". You can tell me something all day long, but I have to personally experience it. I've always been that way and from what I've observed, most people are. We're rebellious creatures, like children who have been told not to touch a hot stove but do it anyway.

I now experienced what sexual sin was as a Christian. Things were different. Before I knew the Lord, my life was filled with all kinds of sin, so it was normal. It's like when a person eats junk food all the time, another bite of it doesn't feel any different in the body. It's used to it. However, once this person gets a taste of healthy food, how clean and pure it makes her feel, and she eats it for years, there is a marked difference when she goes back to junk food. It makes her feel awful. Her body recognizes the toxins, there might be side effects, like a migraine, sore joints or brain fogginess. The difference is palpable. It was the same with me and sexual sin.

When I came to Christ, I felt clean, as if I had just taken a hot shower and got scrubbed, but the sensation of purity stayed with me. There was a difference in the way I felt on a visceral level. Sin and righteousness weren't just something I learned about from a book. They were now a real tug of war inside my heart and soul. I knew what life outside of Christ had to offer, having lived twenty-nine years of it, then four years living with Christ. I went from dark sadness to light happiness and bright hope with Jesus, then back again.

I had fallen again and was devastated. How could this be after I had dedicated my life to Christ? How could I have experienced such power of the Holy Spirit, then shared my testimony of being freed from sexual sin with thousands of people, only to go backwards and do this all over again? I was disgusted with myself. I felt dirty and ashamed. I went back home from the weekend at the premiere depressed, trying to make sense of what I had just done and figure out where I was with God.

During the months and years afterwards, I tried to recover. I confessed my sin to close friends and confidantes, those people within the church whom I knew and trusted. Some supported and loved me, some judged me, some cut ties with me completely. I prayed, had people pray for me, prayed together alongside others. There would be periods of recovery where I would try to turn my heart back to the Lord with all that I had within me, then something would trigger me to fall back again. It seemed like the cycle of self-destruction I had been in since I was fourteen years old bound me tightly.

Before I came to Jesus, it was as if I had been scrambling to climb to the top of a mountain over the course of my whole life. I would have intense endurance towards summiting, getting above the clouds to get a glimpse of the heavens, then would trip and fall, only to slide back down again. I'd pick myself up to scrape and scramble back to return to my previous position. Two steps forward, then one step back or sometimes, five steps forward and eight steps back. Even after coming to Jesus, all my progress seemed to turn into a landslide. I started to do the same thing all over again: go out drinking or meet a guy or a combination of both. If it didn't end up in a man's bed, I drove drunk or passed out somewhere foreign to me. I looked as far from a Christian as possible.

When I came to Christ, I learned that sex is a deeply emotional experience designed by God to take place between a husband and a wife. It is the most intimate act that you can take place between two people and is designed this way in order for a marriage to bond. When this intimacy is outside the confines of a marriage, it confuses the mind and the body. It is a spiritual act, either holy or unholy, clean or dirty. When I was introduced to sex at 14 years old, it was dirty. That is all I knew.

After years of teaching on scriptures through the ministry and hearing the stories of women (and men) who had experienced heartache from sex out of wedlock, the more I understood that it only caused pain. The more I read the Bible, the more I understood that God has designed sex for marriage. Sex outside of marriage is a sin. Sin leads to death. Death is depression: it's dark, it's heartache and much more.

The world teaches differently, of course. Sex is publicized as healthy in every way, shape and form. It's a free-for-all. It's so "not taboo" anymore that everyone is doing it with everyone else. Porn is rampant. Sexual imagery is on the cover of every magazine, splashed over social media and in film. Lust and everything that goes along with it, including porn, fills us temporarily, like popcorn at the movie theater; you can't stop eating it and when you do, you feel sick to your stomach and then empty again. That gauge in our heart which tells us that something is wrong or bad for us is broken.

I chased sex when I was hurting emotionally. I searched for comfort in the midst of disappointment, rejection, and deep sadness. The behavior was ironic, because the rape had brought me anything but solace. I seemed to be always left with the image that I was still that awkward teenager in my Opus sweatshirt being introduced to the boy who said, "No way!" I believed that I wasn't good enough to be loved.

Whether I was in a dating relationship or in a one-night stand, I would try to detach from the emotions and the intimacy with the other person. However, as hard as I tried, I couldn't. I was always left emotionally impacted in one way or another. After having experienced living in both the world and the Kingdom of God, without Christ and with Christ, everything became clearer. I felt gross when I had sex. I felt unclean, filled with shame and sadness and emptier than I was when I fell into the embrace of another man.

What made things worse is that somewhere along the journey, I lost the childlike faith I had in the beginning of my walk. The days of a fresh love and feelings of purity and wholeness had vanished or at least were covered by a thick blanket. Gone were the long walks where He would speak to me, the warm fuzzy feeling like He was cuddling me at night, and the joy unspeakable. I also reached a point where I couldn't even tell if Holy Spirit spoke to me or not. I was truly in darkness during this period, as if my life in Christ had started off as a renaissance, but now I was back to the dark ages.

I believed lies about God and also lies about myself. I believed He didn't protect me from getting hurt or that I could stop this perpetual cycle of sin. I also thought I couldn't pursue Him during this season, that He wouldn't want to be close to me, because I was dirty. Why would He want to cuddle up to an adulterer? The conundrum was that I wanted His presence back so desperately, but I felt so horribly about myself that I couldn't walk away from the sin that kept me from pursuing Him.

I couldn't understand why I hadn't been freed of this destructive cycle, why I couldn't seem to fix it as hard as I tried. I definitely didn't feel or look like a follower of Christ, embroiled in sin, going out with friends to get drunk, and sleeping with men. There was also a lot of anger towards the Lord during these years. Haven't we all been in relationships where we are angry at the other person, but at the same time want them to hold us and tell us that everything is going to be OK? It was like a real fight in marriage.

The church is likened to "the Bride of Christ" in scripture.

When Jesus returns in the book of Revelation (which is set in the future and is yet to come), the Apostle John wrote, "And I heard, as it were, the voice of a great multitude, as the sound of many waters and as the sound of mighty thunderings, saying, 'Alleluia! For the Lord God Omnipotent reigns! Let us be glad and rejoice and give Him glory, for the marriage of the Lamb has come, and His wife has made herself ready.' And to her it was granted to be arrayed in fine linen, clean and bright, for the fine linen is the righteous acts of the saints" (Revelation 19:6-8 NKJV). This Bride is me. This is us, the church.

But I was also the adulterer, turning to other idols in place of Him. The book of Hosea is a picture of a wife who is committing adultery against her husband. This is also a picture of Christ and the church. The Lord says to Hosea, "...Go again, love a woman who is loved by a lover and is committing adultery, just like the love of the LORD for the children of Israel, who look to other gods and love the raisin cakes of the pagans" (Hosea 3:1 NKJV). My idols were the raisin cakes of pseudo-comfort in the arms of other men. I was running from Christ to get comfort, not to Him. Yet, He was relentless in His pursuit of me. He wanted to be my One and Only.

I had blamed God for not protecting me from the pain, but in reality, I was the one walking into destruction time and again. If only I had given Him another chance, let Him heal my heart, things would have been different. But I didn't. With every heartbreak, I would continue to turn back to the familiar. It was a cycle of lies, of unbelief, of bad choices, and ultimately of an old lifestyle.

As far as I ran, I couldn't escape the deep questions that lurked in my heart. They are best laid out in the words of Psalm 77:7-9 (TPT): "Would you really walk off and leave me forever, my Lord God? Won't you show me your kind favor, delighting in me again? Has your well of sweet mercy dried up? Will your promises never come true? Have you somehow forgotten to show me love?"

A few short months after the film premiere, I moved back to Los Angeles and continued to work as an actor. It's funny how God continues to bless us even when we are caught up in muck and mire. In June of 2008, I got cast in a small role on a hit TV show. I was booked on the episode for one week so the cast and crew got pretty comfortable together.

One day while on set, I went to peruse the craft service table to see if I could fill my boredom between scenes with a sugar high from a cookie. While I was there, one of the crew members walked up to me and made a beeline for the very same cookie I had been reaching for. He said, "That's the one I wanted!" We laughed and started talking. He was about six-foot-two, broad shouldered and blue eyed. His name was Troy.

He seemed like a typical "crew guy" on set with tattoos and a rugged demeanor. I can't say that I was initially physically attracted to him, but his strong presence drew me towards him. I felt like he would protect me, not harm me. He asked me if I wanted to go out to get something to eat with him during our lunch break that day. I said yes. We strolled off the studio lot and grabbed a bite to go at a local strip mall, then parked ourselves at a bench where we talked.

Troy struck me as one of the most gentle, kind, and respectful men I ever met. Totally random and unexpected connection. Spending time with him felt like a splash of cool water on a hot day. I needed this in my life.

Over lunch, he stared at me with his huge blue eyes and made clear to me that he was single, that he was interested in me and that he was a one-woman kind of man, meaning that if he liked someone, he only had eyes for her. This candor took me aback.

As usual, a man who respected me was foreign to me. However, it established my trust in him. He was honest and he didn't mince words. I could tell that he really felt that I was special, even though he barely knew me after only a few days working together on set.

The pattern of not being physically attracted to a man who was kind to me initially rang true with him. The lack of attraction wasn't because he wasn't handsome, but because of my own issues stemming from my past, just like with the poet in San Francisco. This time however, it turned into our favor. In the weeks to come when we were dating, I kept our relationship friendly, leaving the physical intimacy out of our interactions together. We learned about each other through talking and spending time together, not through sex, which was completely new to me.

Given my past, I was doubtful that a relationship with him would go anywhere. I was guarded. I'd been hurt and I'd hurt others, and I was tired of it, but I felt safe with Troy. It was clear that he really cared for me and had my best interests at heart. He also provided stability for me

114

in an unstable time in my life. He owned a home, had two young sons, and a stable job.

Over the course of time, I realized he was falling in love with me. His kind of love was unconditional because when he loved someone, he was completely committed. In addition to that, he didn't want to harm me in any way. The more I spent time with him, the more I started to fall for him and the more attractive he became to me. For me, it was a true falling in love, because I fell in love with the person, rather than with the intimacy, which was very different than most all the other men I had dated. It was out of this love that the physical attraction grew.

In many ways, just being with Troy was healing to my heart after all of the pain I'd been through. I had never been in a relationship with a man for more than a handful of months, but this seemed like it could be long-term. I also fell in love with his two little boys. We snuggled on the couch and watched movies. It seemed like I finally had my own family. I had pushed away all the other men who had treated me with kindness and respect, but this one I pulled close. This one I wanted to keep.

The problem was that, even though I wasn't following the Lord at the time, I still wanted to be with a man who loved God and wanted to pursue Him. Troy did not. It was an inner conflict for me: for the first time I had met a man who loved me and treated me like gold, but he wasn't following Jesus. I wanted to date someone who shared the same beliefs, but I also wanted to be with someone I loved and trusted.

Given my pattern over the years, you can probably guess that we eventually became physically intimate. Most of those times would involve alcohol in one form or another. We lived out our lives together the only way we knew how. I was in a loving relationship, but I was not at my best. I knew who I was capable of being, the joyful and peaceful, excited-for-life Simone, because I had experienced her just after I gave my heart to Christ. I craved to walk in that purity again.

My life with Troy was a conundrum. We were in love, I felt safe and protected, we had a family, but we were not pursuing Jesus. About seven months into our relationship, I started to feel a strong pull inside of me back to the Lord. It was also around this time that he dropped a bombshell on me: he told me that he didn't want to have more children.

I was thirty-five years old and I still wanted to have kids. I'd told him that at the beginning of the relationship and he'd said that he was open to the idea. But this new development, the thought of settling down with one man and choosing to never become a mother to my own children, was too much to bear. Having my own kids had been a dream of mine since I was a little girl. The dissonance of it all is that he was the best man I had ever known. He loved me, cherished me and honored me. Yet, the relationship was starting to feel very wrong to me.

This is where pornography entered the picture. I'm not sure what exactly led me to it or how the door was opened, but it had something to do with the relationship I was in. The spiritual element of our lives is so much stronger than we realize.

Throughout the course of our lives, we had both consistently submitted to a spirit of lust, meaning sex outside of marriage. I had opened the doors to lust in so many different ways in my life that I'm surprised that it didn't happen earlier. But now, it was a way of escape. I was running from reality, from pain and brokenness. When I was feeling horrible, particularly about where this relationship was heading, I could get lost in a feeling that gave me a high.

Even though I had experienced drinking and drugs, this was different. No wonder it is called an "addiction." I got hooked on the dopamine being released every time I did it. The internet had become huge, so there it was in my face, an opportunity twenty-four seven. I would be with my boyfriend and then go home and do this. I felt gross, but I couldn't stop myself, and I kept it a secret from my mate.

My life had spiraled out of control. Here I was in a loving relationship, which seemed like everything I had ever wanted, and yet I was still unhappy. I was having sex outside of marriage, and I was addicted to porn. It seemed like everywhere I turned, I couldn't get anything right. I was facing the possibility of not having children and not following God if I stayed with him, but if I left him, we would both be heartbroken. And yet if I got out of this relationship, I reasoned, maybe the cycle of destruction would end, and I could really start following Jesus again.

Over the next couple of months, I started going to church and attending a small fellowship group. I began to read the Bible again every day and listen to worship music. I even went on my first ten day, all liquid fast in hopes of gaining spiritual strength and clarity. I just couldn't shake the feeling that this relationship was wrong. Everything in me was feeling like I needed to leave the relationship and pursue the Lord full time again. But I loved this man and didn't want to leave.

One night in the Spring of 2009, while falling asleep next to Troy, I had a dream when I was half asleep. I saw Jesus come to me in a white robe with his arms reaching out to me. He was motioning me to come back to Him, back into His arms. I walked towards Him and He held me tightly. When I woke up the next morning, I knew that I had to walk away from this man. For the first time in my life, I had found genuine love with another man. Now I had to leave him so I could fully follow Jesus again.

I showed up at Troy's house one evening with a grocery bag full of his random items of clothing and other things of his I had collected over our year long relationship. He let me inside and we sat on his couch. I told him that I couldn't go on, that I was ending it because I wanted to have children of my own. That was partially true, but the reality was that I didn't know how to explain to a man who didn't know Jesus that God was leading me away from the relationship.

With tears in his eyes, he begged me not to leave him, saying that he loved me and wanted to spend the rest of his life with me. My heart was torn in two: stay with this man I loved or follow my dreams and follow God. I simply couldn't ignore the strong pull in my gut to walk away and begin to pursue God passionately again. Sure, I wanted to be married, I wanted this type of relationship, I wanted a man very similar to this one I was in love with, but I wanted us to live a Christian life together and that wasn't going to happen in its present state. As much as I wanted to stay, I was drawn out of that house, leaving him and his kids behind.

That night I broke up with him was a few days after the one-year anniversary of our first official date. My heart was shattered. I drove away pouring my heart out to the Lord in tears and went straight to my friend's house where she and her husband prayed for me. We prayed for the Lord to wrap His arms around Troy and the boys and not let them go, to bring them to Him, into His fold, just like He had done for me. They prayed for me, that the Lord would heal my broken heart and place me on the path that He had set before me. After I left my friend's house, I remember the moment I gave it all over to God. I pulled up at a certain stoplight near my apartment at approximately 9 p.m. I prayed, "OK, Lord, I gave him up to follow You, so please promise me that You will bring me my husband and that I will be married someday soon."

Chapter 8

Engaged: "to be interlocked; to be bound; to be meshed together"

After the break-up with Troy, I immediately dove into the things of God and began to passionately pursue Him again. I was the hungriest for Him that I had been since I came to the Lord. However, now that I was single in my mid-30's, I started to think about my age, having kids, and I became preoccupied about marriage. The relationship I had just gotten out of gave me a taste of what relationship and family was all about. I believed I was ready.

I had wanted to get married since I was a little girl. When I was in my twenties, I was trying to figure life out and just make it through. I also hadn't really met anyone that I would have considered "husband material." After I gave my heart to the Lord at twenty-nine, the desire for marriage started to grow in my heart. I wanted to be loved and I wanted to love somebody. I wanted to settle down with one person and to stop the roller coaster I was on with men for years. Since I had never been in a long-term relationship before Troy, the experience of being in that relationship for the previous year gave me a taste of what that feels like.

I also knew the scripture 1 Corinthians 7:8-9 NKJV, in which Apostle Paul writes, "But I say to the unmarried and to the widows: It is good for them if they remain even as I am; but if they cannot exercise self-control, let them marry. For it is better to marry than to burn with passion." If I wanted to be intimate with a man, I should be in covenant. I had been physical with many men, but never in marriage. I wanted to know what that was like, what it means to be married. The Lord was giving me a fresh start in my life and I wanted to experience a relationship with a man God's way, not mine.

Like many other single men and women in this day and age, I went online to meet a man. I was looking for a man who was around my age (mid-thirties), who was ready to get married and have children, who loved the Lord and pursued Him, who had similar dreams as I had (to be in ministry), who was funny and made me laugh, who loved to be outdoors, liked sports and being in the mountains. There is more to that list, but I could go on and on. I dated a few people here and there, but nothing fit.

Almost six months to the day after my crushing breakup with Troy, I connected with Jonah, a single pastor at a local church. He was everything that I wrote about above. We wrote back and forth through the dating site and we had so much in common. Since we lived so close to each other (within a mile, which is unusual in sprawling Los Angeles), that we arranged to meet quickly, so we could see if we were right for each other.

We met for a beer at a local pub one night. He had dark features and was relatively handsome with a rugged, almost lumberjack look about him. But it was his personality that drew me in. He was hysterically funny. Laughter was so needed for me after my break-up the summer before this December meeting. We talked about so many facets of our lives, our dreams, our goals and most importantly, our love for Jesus, which was so different than my last relationship. He also met my intellectual needs because he was a deep thinker, but it was balanced out with a silly sense of humor. I felt so free with him. During that first meeting, we closed the place down after losing track of time in our deep conversation.

Within a few short weeks, we fell for each other. It all happened very quickly, but I had often heard it said that when people are older, it's easier to know when someone is right for us, because we know what we want and what we don't want out of a mate. Jonah checked off all of my boxes of what I wanted, and He told me that he had found the woman he wanted to marry.

I met his family and they also seemed solid and grounded in their faith in Christ. His mother had told me that if she were to have a picture of everything he had wanted and prayed for in a woman, it would have been me. We spent our courtship talking for hours about God, about what He was doing in our lives, and what our goals and dreams were.

We were also both public speakers.

He was a pastor, and I had traveled the country speaking in ministry, so we wanted to continue on that path. I was still acting, but I ached to get back to ministry across the country and around the world. We also both wanted to travel on missions' trips. This was so different from my last relationship, in which I was the only one who wanted to pursue God. I also felt the peace of Holy Spirit about being with him, one in which I sensed the Father looking down on us and smiling at our coming together. I fell in love with Jonah and he with me, and so it was a time of great joy. It was so nice for me to experience that after such a long period of turmoil.

After three months of dating, he asked me to go on a hike with him. We loved the mountains and hiking this route had been "our thing," so nothing about it was out of the ordinary. At the summit, we took on the view on that crisp, cool morning. Somehow, he had gotten me to turn around and when I turned back, he was on his knee, flowers in one hand and a small black box in the other.

"This is happening, this is really happening!" That must be what most women are thinking when they are proposed to. I felt like God was answering the prayer I had said the year before, driving home from my ex-boyfriend's house after walking out, the one in which I asked for a husband. After all of the junk I had been through, the Lord was redeeming my past yet again.

I'd never been excited about the thought of planning a wedding. I thought they were a waste of money and had always wanted a small one.

But with Jonah, the prospect of a big wedding seemed fun. Always the life of the party, he wanted no less than ten groomsmen. Jonah always made things fun and he brought out some of the best in me, so I decided to just let my creative side out and have fun too. After all, I was only going to get married once!

I planned all the perfect details for my wedding. The dress came first, as it usually does with a woman. I'd gone into a local store with some friends and tried a slew of various choices on, but just like on television, I knew "the one" when I slipped it on. It was an ivory colored strapless dress with a beaded corset and a huge puffy skirt that ended in a train that stretched for several feet. It made me feel like a princess. I felt like a bride, clean and pure. My fiancé on the other hand, wanted all the groomsmen to be in Chuck Taylor Converse shoes, so I decided to add some spice and put myself and all the ladies in them too. It reflected our quirky sense of humor, which I loved adding into the mix. My bridesmaids would be wearing chocolate brown dresses, chosen because of the scenery in the background behind our ceremony.

We booked the most breathtaking venue on a lake nestled in the Eastern Sierra mountains of California. I grew up going there in the summers as a little girl. In many ways, it felt like a return back to my childhood when my love of being outdoors in the mountains began with the smell of fresh air, hiking, mountains lying before me, while getting dirty and being real.

It would be a Fall wedding, so the aspen trees would be in their glorious splendor bursting with yellows and reds and all shades in between. Aspen trees have always spoken to me because their leaves look like they are shimmering and clapping for me when I walk by them. They are also special to me because my dad and I both love them. Being surrounded by them on my wedding day just felt right.

All the details were coming together. I was going to be married and I could hardly believe it. The idea of me being in a secure relationship with just one man for the rest of my life felt safe and assuring. However, the closer it got to our wedding, I started to feel anxious. It wasn't a fear of getting married, but of being abandoned. I'd not felt this in my previous relationship, but I did with Jonah. During my sleep on several nights, I dreamed that he would break up with me and I would be heartbroken. Some mornings I would wake up from these dreams in tears.

In spite of the security of being engaged to a man who loved me, I was so scared of getting my heart broken and this would lead to me being nearly physically paralyzed with fear. It overcame me like a real physical attack. There were days when I felt like I could barely get anything done, like my mind and body were numb.

I knew something was wrong with me. I needed professional help, some sort of deep inner healing. I knew that my fear of abandonment was birthed out of the events of my past.

I shared these dreams and fears with my fiancé. We were going to be married, after all, so I was honest and transparent. I told him that I felt like I was being tormented and I needed to get counseling to work through this. He responded by praying for me and assuring me that he was not going to leave, saying that he loved me and was going to marry me. I still battled.

It was a hot summer day in my 600 square foot studio apartment when my fiancé showed up unannounced. He asked if we could go for a walk. He never did that.

Something didn't feel right. I asked him what was wrong, but he implored me to go for a walk. I said no, please say what you're going to say here and now. He said he couldn't do it, he couldn't go through with the wedding. Did that mean postponing it, I asked? He said no, that he decided that he didn't want to marry me. He was ending it. He wasn't just canceling the wedding, he was breaking off our relationship entirely. I felt like I was punched in the gut and the wind was knocked out of me.

The venue had been booked, the dress had been purchased, the invitations had been sent out, and people had purchased their plane tickets for this destination wedding. My whole life flashed before me in that moment. I asked why. He didn't have a reason, except that it just didn't feel right.

We ended up going on that walk and my tears flowed. He wanted to comfort me, but also didn't want to get too close. He was cold and seemed indifferent. To this day, I have no idea what shifted in him, why he changed. Maybe it was all the fear that I was experiencing, or maybe that fear was a warning to me that this would happen, or maybe he just had cold feet. All I knew at the time was that I couldn't wrap my head around this tremendous loss.

In the months following, I begged him to come back. I wrote emails, texts, and made phone calls, but he never did. He had turned around and walked away for good. I was devastated. To make matters worse, in my grief I had to call and cancel the wedding venue and tell my friends to try and get refunds on their travel plans. It was a nightmare.

I fell on my knees before God and screamed, "Why didn't you protect my heart?!?!"

I felt dead inside. I had experienced deep rejection and abandonment from this man whom I had trusted enough to agree to marry. The old lie was whispered in my ear, "You're not good enough." I tried to press into God. I went to church, I met with the pastor, I met with friends, I prayed and had people pray for me, but it was so incredibly difficult. I was angry. At him and at God. I had hoped that He would protect me from this kind of pain. I'd had such a peace about marrying Jonah.

In retrospect, I thought that getting married would be the answer to the painful issues I was still dealing with. My anxiety and fears about him leaving me came from past rejection. I had given my heart to someone completely and I was so scared that he would break it. But I had never dealt with the root cause of my issues. Then the engagement happened and a few weeks in, they started to rear their ugly heads. I knew I needed help to sort through my thoughts and feelings, but I hadn't known where to turn.

It's in our human nature to think that "band aids" will heal our wounds. We choose anything that will temporarily placate the pain, without going through the hard trenches of facing our issues. The truth is, covering them up will not heal them. They will only heal from the inside out. I'd placed proverbial band-aids all over my wounds for years and they were clearly not helping me. But how could I get to a place of victory?

I had dealt with years of pain and rejection, self-destructive behavior, and sexual abuse. I needed to be with Jesus full-time, all the time. But again, I looked outside of Him for fulfillment and sought out a relationship. Just as the harlot wife in the book of Hosea, I would continue to turn to those "delicious raisin cakes" that temporarily comforted me so much.

It wasn't long after the break-up before I fell headlong back into old patterns of self-sabotage and destruction. This time, it was as bad as it ever was. I had been a server at a restaurant as I pursued my acting career. My coworkers found out what had happened with the ending of my engagement and did their best to console me. In many ways, they were more supportive than the church body was at the time. Christians would listen to me share with them about my heartache and pray for me, but the employees at my job got me out and about. Unfortunately, this meant taking me to bars and drinking. The truth is, I did need to get out and about to do things, but given my history with alcohol, this was the worst place I could be spending my time, especially during an intense period of heartache.

It's no surprise that I stepped right back into my old patterns of drinking and men. It was like these two demons were always waiting there for me, beckoning my return to the ways of living that I had tried so hard to escape. I got into a relationship with yet another man who was completely opposite of everything I stood for. My drinking reached a point where I would drive home drunk on a regular basis. How I was never pulled over and arrested is a mystery to me. It should have happened countless times, but I was spared.

I was in a very dark place. The more I drank, the deeper I would sink into depression. And truth be told, now that I understand who Satan is and how he only wants to kill, steal and destroy, I can see clearly in hindsight that he was trying to grab hold of me and ruin my life. What happened to the woman who traveled the country sharing her testimony, preaching the gospel and leading people to Christ? What happened to the woman who stood for sexual purity after so many years of self-destruction? That woman had fallen right back into all of it, and it felt like there was no way out. I had given my life to Christ and my life still looked the same. What was going on?

My honeymoon had been booked to travel to a remote village of Switzerland, since the two of us loved the mountains so much. So, after the engagement ended, I was stuck with a trip to Europe and nobody to go with. I'd mentioned this in passing to a girl I worked with. She's a travel bug and is up for flying anywhere on a moment's notice. When she heard that I was looking for a vacation buddy, she jumped at the chance.

Flash forward a few weeks later and we were in Paris drinking a bottle of wine. She is a sweet woman and truly cared about my hurting heart. I remember her hugging me in the backroom of the restaurant right after he broke-up with me. Then here we were, two women on Easter weekend in arguably, the most beautiful city in the world.

We arranged to stay with a friend of my parents. She was an older French woman who had a gorgeous flat in the heart of the Montmarte district. We could see the Eiffel Tower outside of our bedroom window. It was heavenly.

My friend and I talked for hours about the break-up, what happened, and how I could get through it. She is not a Christian, so the conversation was not centered around Christ or Biblical principles, but she supported me in my faith and allowed me to unleash everything that I was thinking and feeling with her as they bubbled up inside me.

We walked around the city, taking in the architecture, the sound of the French language, the food, and the wine. We drank our way through one of the most breathtaking cities in the world.

I'd been to Paris several times before. It's where I learned about my fear of heights and here I was, some 25 years later, a completely different person. I'd initially thought my trip would be more of an "eat, pray, love" trip where I would go alone and explore the city on my own and reconnect with the Lord. I'd imagined that this time alone with Him would be very healing. But when my friend decided to come with me, everything changed. The worst was coming out of me.

We were drunk every night of our vacation and on most nights, I blacked out. With the alcohol came depression. It was like a roller coaster. I'd wake up in the morning, foggy from the night before and feeling horrible about myself. Then midday or afternoon would roll around and we would start again. The sadness would lift off my mind and my heart and we would be light and carefree.

It was anything but freedom. I was locked into my self-destructive behavior again. Furthermore, it was happening in one of my favorite cities, far away from my "real life". However, there were fleeting moments when I longed to be that child who was climbing the stairs of the Tower with her Dad. I would have given anything to press the reset button on my life. I just wanted to be someone else.

On the last night we were there, we met up with another friend of ours who just happened to be in the city at the same time. We started drinking and chain-smoking. Somehow, I ended up giving my credit card to someone at a bar to charge a $500 bill. It was way out of my budget at the time.

The three of us took a cab back to the flat where we were staying. My mom's friend was fast asleep in her room. We were drunk out of our minds and two of us passed out. My friend who was staying with me, packed up all of our belongings, because we had to be at the airport in a few short hours. The problem was, we couldn't move.

The noise must have woken up the sweet woman who so graciously housed us. She came out of her room and to her shock, there were two people (myself and our male friend) passed out on the floor, while my roommate tried to console her. She was angry.

The memories are blurry, as I try to piece together that morning, but when I arrived at the airport, I had missed my flight. I had to negotiate in a foggy, slurred speech with the French customer service agent to pay extra to be scheduled on another one. I remember the look of disgust on her face. I was clearly still inebriated.

When we got home and went to work, the stories of our Paris shenanigans made people laugh. They thought it sounded like I had an amazing time, but truthfully, I was nearing my rock bottom. I'd made a fool of myself throughout that city, ruined a beautiful friendship with my host, lost more money than I had budgeted to spend, and truly felt dirty. I was disgusted by my behavior and who I had become, but I continued.

I didn't know how to stop my behavior. I'd had so many "rock-bottoms" during and after Paris, but one stands out in my memory in particular. I was out one night at a birthday party for a co-worker in Downtown Los Angeles. As I mentioned previously, I had a problem with drinking and driving. I drank way too much alcohol and got into my car to drive myself home. After getting lost and driving down a one-way street, I got onto the highway praying that I wouldn't get pulled over and get a DUI. The thought of the possibility of killing myself or someone else on the journey didn't even occur to me until after the fact. Of course, Los Angeles freeways are difficult to maneuver sober, let alone drunk. But I made it. It was pretty much a miracle.

As I made my final approach to my apartment and pulled onto the side street, I started to cry. When I say cry, I mean bawl, like everything from all of my years was bubbling up and gushing out in screaming, guttural cries. Within my grief, while my eyes were shut, I saw a vision of God Himself bringing me home safely that night. In spite of my wretched sin and turning away while blaming Him for all of my woes, He was still navigating me and taking care of me.

I felt as though they were the cries of deep repentance from a place in my heart where I had blamed the Lord for all of the pain that I experienced. They were also cries asking for forgiveness from all my years of turning to other "idols" to fulfill me, heal me, and comfort me. His Word says, "You shall have no other gods before Me" (Exodus 20:3 NKJV). But I did have many "gods," or idols. I turned to them for comfort, instead of turning to the One who truly wanted to change me from the inside out. On that alcohol saturated night, He was trying to get me home to Him safely all along the journey of my life.

A few months after returning home from Paris, I was taking an acting class. One night, I got into a conversation with the teacher about her history with alcoholism. I ended up staying with her for hours after the other students left just to listen to her story. What she shared with me was very similar to my past with drinking. I found out that a symptom of alcoholism is getting blackout drunk, which had been happening since I was a young teenager. It never occurred to me that I could be an alcoholic, but I was willing to find out.

The next day, she took me to an Alcoholics Anonymous meeting. I was more than ready to go, but I felt out of place while I was there. I knew I had a problem with alcohol, but I still wasn't certain that I was ready to admit that I was an alcoholic. I also didn't believe that AA was where I was going to get the inner healing I so desperately needed. It seemed so structured and uncomfortable. So, I attended only a handful of meetings, but it was enough to get me on a path of sobriety that lasted more than a year.

After truly repenting, or turning away from my sinful behavior, I believed the Lord responded to my heart's cry by pouring out His grace to strengthen me to stay sober. The scripture that says, "I can do all things through Christ who strengthens me," never rang truer for me than during this time (Philippians 4:13 NKJV). Eliminating the drinking stopped the sexual promiscuity. It was the one act of quitting alcohol that gave me the clarity and strength to turn back to God.

There is one thing that I have learned about life, especially in walking with the Lord: there is always the opportunity for a "do-over," meaning He keeps giving us fresh starts over and over again. Like the dawn of a fresh morning, crisp and cool, clear and bright, with hope and a sense of renewal in my heart, my life was about to change.

Chapter 9

Healing: "to make sound or whole; to restore to health; to restore to original purity or integrity"

I was desperate for someone to come alongside me and help me break the cycle of destruction I was always falling back into. In the past, I had thought that if I talked to a therapist long enough, I would get over my issues. I went to countless counseling sessions, but nobody helped me permanently change my ways. What I needed was a person who would not only listen to all that I had gone through in my life, but walk me through the process of inner healing, teaching me practical tools to keep me from repeatedly going through the same patterns. Every time I went back to following and serving the Lord, I never trusted myself not to go back to my old ways. I made a decision to find someone who could meet both of these needs. By God's grace I found a woman who could help me, so I began to see her on a bi-weekly basis.

She wasn't just any counselor with a degree or certificate just to listen to problems. She knew the Word of God through and through and was filled with the Holy Spirit. She had also gone through sexual assault and trauma in her life and had received inner healing herself, so she had a great deal of empathy for me. Needless to say, she was experienced and knowledgeable about helping people get set free from bondage to sin.

As I started to meet with this therapist on a regular basis, I began the journey of inner healing that I so desperately needed. I'd met her a couple of years prior and had made appointments with her sporadically, but I'd been only half-heartedly committed to giving up my sin until this point. However, I had since hit rock bottom and was determined to never again circle around the destructive patterns I had been trapped in for so many years.

The term "inner healing" was something that I'd heard a lot in the church. It's rooted in the idea that we are wounded by events or traumas that have happened to us and words that have been spoken over us (or that we have spoken over ourselves). The healing part of the term is the means of effectively dealing with these events or words and their repercussions manifesting in the present, so there will be lasting change in the future.

It is out of the hurt of emotional wounds that we act out in our own lives. For example, in the aftermath of being raped at fourteen years old, I acted out of that pain through drinking, sexual promiscuity and starving myself. Even though I gave my heart to Christ and was saved, I wasn't healed nor could I stop the actions that continued to come back into my life. The only way to break this cycle was to get inner healing from those wounds so that I wouldn't respond to them with sin anymore.

She offered practical and easy solutions to walk through this process. We worked together and identified lies that I believed, established my identity in Christ, forgave people, and repented from idols. This type of prayer and repentance is also a form of deliverance. The definition of deliverance is "the action of being rescued or set free" (Google). The devil had me locked in a prison to sin through several avenues. These inroads needed to be cut off at the pass.

Ultimately, my mind needed to be renewed from the lies I believed about myself. "And do not be conformed to this world, but be transformed by the renewing of your mind, that you may prove what is that good and acceptable and perfect will of God." For years, I had been shaped and molded to this world and its ways of coping with pain, whether it was using sex, alcohol, or an eating disorder. My mind needed to be renewed and I desperately wanted to be transformed into a new woman.

Lies:

Actions taken towards us or against us can cause us to believe lies about ourselves. And when we believe a lie, we act in response to that lie. "Don't you know that when you allow even a little lie into your heart, it can permeate your entire belief system?" (Gal. 5:9 TPT) When the boy rejected me at the arcade that one afternoon back in the '80s, I started to believe, "I'm not good enough." That's a lie that was compounded with the countless times I was rejected over the course of my life. It became a life theme and continued to haunt me through the ending of my engagement and beyond.

After I was raped, I believed the lie that I was worthless, so for years I treated myself like I was worthless. This was coupled with the lie that I was "unlovable" which grew larger and more powerful over time. Because I believed that I wasn't loved, I desperately sought it out in different ways. I treated myself with disrespect, sleeping with men in hopes that they would somehow love me.

This lie about love persisted even after I came to Christ. I knew Jesus loved me and I had felt His love in a tangible way for many years. But when I wasn't feeling it, I turned to men.

It was out of this old lie that I also developed an unbalanced desire to be married after I came to Christ. It almost became an obsession. Many people want to get married, but for me, more than anything, I was desperate to be loved. I thought that if I got married, I would be permanently loved and never abandoned or lonely anymore. The breakup of my engagement when I was essentially "left at the altar" only fueled the existing lie that I was unlovable. This fixation on marriage tormented me for several years afterwards.

I also believed that I was always overlooked, that I wasn't good enough or worthy to be married. I thought that God thought the same things, because I would be married if He thought otherwise. So, I chased after marriage, thinking that I could make it happen, rather than just letting God orchestrate it. I was so desperate I could barely breathe sometimes. The lies that I believed were affecting my behavior, my choices, and ultimately, the quality of my life.

From the rape onward, I believed that I was alone in what I was going through. This caused me to experience the feeling of loneliness. Out of loneliness, I sought companionship, many times unhealthy companionship.

Words that are spoken over us can also be the seeds for lies we believe. People in high school called me a slut behind my back after the rape and I believed this lie as well. When my first talent agent told me that I was "plus size," I believed I was fat, ugly, and again that I wasn't "good enough" to be accepted into the acting and modeling industry. The response to this lie was to starve myself. I beat my body into submission so I could be accepted.

Lies are powerful and they come from Satan. He is called "the father of lies" in John 8:44, and he wants to keep us in a dark place, just like I had been for years. It was a lie that led Eve to take a bite of fruit in the Garden of Eden. The devil said to her, "[If you eat it] you will not surely die. For God knows that in the day you eat of it your eyes will be opened, and you will be like God, knowing good and evil" (Genesis 3:4-5 NKJV). That was the exact opposite of what God had told her. Because she believed what the serpent told her, rather than believing the Word of God, she ate the fruit, sinned, and lived the rest of her life separated from God. This is a clear picture of how we act in response to lies.

In order to break the cycle of our destructive, sinful actions, we have to stop believing the lies that fuel them. That seemed impossible to me. How was I going to just stop believing these lies that I believed for years?

During my counseling sessions, I learned how to renounce the lies and replace them with truth. We would pray to dig deep into my mind and my soul and ask God to reveal to me which lies I believed about myself and about my life. When the lies came to mind, my counselor led me in prayer to renounce them one by one. The definition of "renounce" is, "to give up, refuse, or resign usually by formal declaration; to refuse to follow, obey, or recognize any further" (Merriam-Webster).

Once we renounced the lies, we spoke out God's truth to replace the lies. Words are powerful. Proverbs 18:21 NKJV says, "Death and life are in the power of the tongue, and those who love it will eat its fruit." I learned that words, both positive and negative, carry much power. Speaking out that I no longer believed these lies was mighty.

This process is best explained by describing a vision I had during one of our sessions. As we were in prayer, I saw that my soul had diverticulitis. This medical condition happens when there are pockets in the intestine where debris, things such as seeds and other food particles, fill and clog. This can cause infection. I saw that the same thing was happening in my soul. Lies were stuck in many places in my soul and infection ran rampant. I was sick. If I renounced the lies, the "seeds" that were causing an "infection," would be popped out. I also saw that once these pockets were empty, they needed to be filled up with something to replace those "seeds" or "lies," or they would continue to get lodged in them. If I spoke God's Word into these pockets, His truths would fill those pockets in my soul, blocking the lies from ever returning.

When a lie came to my mind, such as, "You're unlovable," I would say, "I renounce the lie that I am unlovable and in its place I declare and decree that 'I am loved with an everlasting love'" (Jeremiah 31:3). Some of the truths were principles, like Jesus' dying on the cross, so that I could be accepted into the Kingdom of Heaven. The lie "I am rejected" was renounced and replaced with, "I am accepted by Jesus, the One who died for my sins." I would speak out any biblical truth or scripture that would come to my mind to replace the lies. Another was that "I am fat," and that was replaced with, "I am fearfully and wonderfully made and perfectly crafted in my mother's womb" (Psalm 139:13-14). And on and on.

The one lie that I believed for almost as long as I could remember was, "I'm not good enough." There were so many scriptures that the Bible has to battle against this one, but the one that I used the most was, "I am more than a conqueror in Christ" (Romans 8:37). Not only did it speak to being "good enough," but it establishes that I am so "good enough" that I am a conqueror with Him by my side. Powerful.

Thankfully, I knew the scriptures well enough by then to know the truth about God and what He thinks of me. When I did not know which truth to replace the lies with, my therapist was there to help me. It was a matter of fitting that truth into those places in my soul where lies had been embedded for so long. I was renewing my mind and transforming my life with truth, but the key was to speak it out loud, just like the Father did when He created the universe. If He spoke life into existence, then as His children, we should follow suit.

Identity:

Oxford Dictionary defines the word "identity" as, "the fact of being who or what a person or thing is." God calls Himself "Yahweh" or "I AM," meaning to exist or to be. The meaning implies that He is solid and immovable. He knows who He is and He is who He is. Have you ever met a person who was so secure in his or her own identity that he or she was virtually unshakable during the trials of life? That is who God is, and it is His hope for us to become like this as well.

Many of us spend our whole lives without solid knowledge of our identity. Identity isn't just a role we assume such as mother, daughter, wife, athlete, etc. It goes beyond that. It's who God created us to be. When we know our identity in Christ, it forms our actions and the choices we make. It changes everything.

When we identify ourselves as anything other than who God created us to be, then we will act out of that identity. Lies and identity are intricately connected. Most of the lies I believed were directly connected to who I believed I was. These lies about our identity start with two words: "I am." Lies such as "I am unlovable, I am a slut, I am worthless, I am not good enough, I am fat, I am ugly, I am overlooked, I am forgotten, I am a failure." These are just a few of the ways we identify ourselves, and we act out of who we believe that we are.

I prayed and asked Holy Spirit to show me what I believed about myself. He revealed that there was much contradiction to what I thought about myself and what He said about me in His Word. I needed to wipe the slate clean with my identity by eradicating my old mindset and replacing it with a new one in Christ. Thankfully, the Bible is filled with thousands of truths about who He says we are, so I went back to those words in my quiet time with Him and spoke them over myself one by one. If I was at a loss of what they were, I did a simple internet search for "my identity in Christ" and countless scriptures popped up. Here are a few examples:

False Identity: "I am ugly. I am fat." **True Identity**: "For we are His workmanship, created in Christ Jesus for good works, which God prepared beforehand that we should walk in them." (Eph. 2:10 NKJV). "Or do you not know that your body is the temple of the Holy Spirit who is in you, whom you have from God, and you are not your own? For you were bought at a price; therefore glorify God in your body and in your spirit, which are God's." (1 Cor. 6:19 NKJV). "I will praise You, for I am fearfully and wonderfully made; marvelous are Your works, and my soul knows very well." (Psalm 139:14 NKJV). I am handcrafted by God. He thought about my every detail before He wove me together in my mother's womb.

False Identity: "I am unwanted. I am unworthy." **True Identity**: "For as many as are led by the Spirit of God, these are sons of God. For you did not receive the spirit of bondage again to fear, but you received the Spirit of adoption by whom we cry out, 'Abba, Father.' The Spirit Himself bears witness with our spirit that we are children of God, and if children then heirs– heirs of God and joint heirs with Christ, if indeed we suffer with Him, that we may also be glorified together." (Romans 8:14-17 NKJV). I am a child of God. I am adopted. I am an heir with Christ.

False Identity: "I am a slut. I am dirty." **True Identity**: "I am the true vine, and My Father is the vinedresser. Every branch in Me that does not bear fruit He takes away; and every branch that bears fruit He prunes, that it may bear more fruit. You are already clean because of the word which I have spoken to you. Abide in Me, and I in you." (John 15:1-4 NKJV). "Therefore, if anyone is in Christ, he is a new creation; old things have passed away; behold, all things have become new." (2 Cor. 5:17 NKJV). I am cared for and tended to by my Heavenly Father. I am clean. I am pure. I am new.

False Identity: "I am overlooked. I am forgotten." **True Identity**: "How precious also are Your thoughts to me, O God! How great is the sum of them! If I should count them, they would be more in number than the sand." (Psalm 139:17-18 NKJV). "I will never leave you nor forsake you." (Deut. 31:6 and Heb. 13:5). He thinks about me all the time. I am precious to Him and He does not forget me or leave me.

False Identity: "I am a failure. I'm not good enough." **True Identity**: "And they overcame him (the devil) by the blood of the Lamb and by the word of their testimony, and they did not love their lives to the death." (Revelation 12:11 NKJV). "Yet in all these things we are more than conquerors through Him who loved us." (Romans 8:37 NKJV). I am an overcomer. I am a conqueror. Because of His blood, I am worthy.

False Identity: "I am unloved." **True Identity**: "Yes, I have loved you with an everlasting love; Therefore, with loving kindness I have drawn you." (Jeremiah 31:3 NKJV). "But God, who is rich in mercy, because of His great love with which He loved us, even when we were dead in trespasses, made us alive together with Christ." (Ephesians 2:4 NKJV). "For this is how much God loved the world-He gave His one and only, unique Son as a gift. So now everyone who believes in Him will never perish but experience everlasting life." (John 3:16 TPT). He loves me. He died for me. I am loved with a great and everlasting love.

When the old identity tries to creep back in, I return to these scriptures and remind myself (and the devil) of who I am in Christ, what my identity is in Him. Once again, the same scripture rings true, "Therefore, if anyone is in Christ, he is a new creation; old things have passed away; behold, all things have become new." (2 Corinthians 5:17 NKJV). The old has gone and the new has come. It's been a powerful change for me. I have become much more solid and secure woman in my healthy, God-ordained identity, and am now making choices accordingly.

Forgiveness:

Forgiveness was an action I needed to take in order to move forward in the process of healing. There was a laundry list of people I needed to forgive in my life and I, Simone, was at the top of it. I needed to forgive myself for all the abuse I put myself through. It was not my fault that I did not know how to stop myself from the cycle of self-destruction I'd been in for so many years.

Jesus forgave on the cross while He was hanging there to die. If He could do it, so could I. "Then Jesus said, 'Father, forgive them, for they do not know what they do.'" (Luke 23:34 NKJV). I had to forgive, because Christ died on the cross to forgive me of my sin.

I had to make an effort to partner with God to change my life. He could change me from the inside out, but I had to be obedient to His Word and do what I could to change. Forgiveness was part of this process. In talking with my counselor in our sessions, during my prayer time with her, and at my home, I asked the Lord to show me who I needed to forgive in my life.

Colossians 3:12-13 NKJV says, "Therefore, as the elect of God, holy and beloved, put on tender mercies, kindness, humility, meekness, long-suffering; bearing with one another, and forgiving one another, if anyone has a complaint against another; even as Christ forgave you, so you must also do." The unforgiveness made me an angry person. Every time I would think of someone who hurt me or offended me in some way, I would feel anger bubble up inside of me.

Forgiveness isn't for the other person (although that is part of it), it's for us. Unforgiveness releases bitterness within us. This causes us to act out in destructive ways, just like I had done for so many years. Forgiveness is not a feeling. Our mouths can forgive, but it takes time for our hearts to go along with it. If we waited until we felt like forgiving everyone we needed to forgive, it would never happen.

I remember learning this principle with my ex-fiancé. I knew I was "supposed" to forgive him, that it's what God said to do, but it was tough. It was actually easier to forgive the man who had raped me, because he had been out of my life for over twenty years. It was more difficult to forgive someone (a pastor, no less) who had essentially left me at the altar less than a year earlier, but I had to do it. It was a process, but I believed that it would help free me from the cycle of anger and bitterness.

I couldn't count how many times I had to verbally, out loud, forgive him and others, but it was a lot and went on for months and in some cases, years. As many people as God brought to mind, I forgave out loud. Again, it was so important to verbalize forgiveness, just as it had been important to declare God's will and truth out of my mouth. Every time I would have a negative thought or a feeling of anger come to me, I'd say, "Lord, I forgive this person (and say his or her name)."

We've probably all heard the phrase, "Hurt people hurt people." It's true. Jesus has a heart of compassion and He understands that we react out of pain. When others are dealing with their own issues of abandonment, rejection, insecurity, lies, and abuse, they will react, just as we all do out of pain. When we forgive them, it changes our heart. It also opens up the door for us to be able to help them, love them, and pray for them, just like Jesus did with the two thieves on the crosses next to Him.

I recently went through a situation in which a co-worker was telling lies about me, spreading them around for others to hear and turning others against me. Using this principle of forgiveness, I quickly forgave her. I could have chosen to be angry or bitter towards her, but the forgiveness allowed me to have compassion on her. I could see that she was acting in many ways like I had before I was healed.

Afterward, God opened the door for me to treat her kindly and help her in any way that I could. I saw that her countenance changed when I did this. It was the love of Jesus flowing from my heart. But unforgiveness blocks that from happening. Had I not forgiven her, I would have still carried bitterness toward her and would not have been free for God to use me in her life. We are now close friends.

As I forgave people one by one, I felt more and more freedom. It literally felt like a weight lifted off of my shoulders. The feelings of forgiveness and peace didn't come right away, but they did come eventually. And as life moved on, God did other amazing things in my life, which also helped me forgive and almost forget what had happened to me. Paul writes in Philippians 3:12-14 NKJV, "Not that I have already attained, or am perfected; but I press on, that I may lay hold of that for which Christ Jesus has also laid hold of me. Brethren, I do not count myself to have apprehended; but one thing I do, forgetting those things which are behind and reaching forward to those things which are ahead, I press toward the goal for the prize of the upward call of God in Christ Jesus." In the same way I was able to forget about my past and move forward towards God's call on my life.

Idols:

The definition of an idol is "an image or representation of a god used as an object of worship" (Oxford). An idol can be something that you turn to for comfort and solace instead of turning to God. It becomes a substitute for Him. Moses walked away from the Israelites to go up to the mountaintop on Mount Sinai with God. This is where God gave him the ten commandments which included, "You shall have no other gods before Me. You shall not make for yourself a carved image– any likeness of anything that is in heaven above, or that is in the earth beneath, or that is in the water under the earth; you shall not bow down to them nor serve them" (Exodus 20: 3-5 NKJV). Ironically, it was while he was up there, listening to His direction for His people, that the Israelites created an idol of their own.

While Moses was on the mountain with God, the Israelites thought they had been abandoned by him and wanted something to worship, wanted a leader. Aaron (his brother) suggested they melt down golden earrings and create a calf. "Then they said, 'This is your god, O Israel, that brought you out of the land of Egypt!'" (Ex. 32:4 NKJV). Actually, God had brought them out of Egypt using Moses as their guide, so this wasn't true. But in his absence, they made up a new story to comfort themselves. They wanted to turn to something, anything they could believe in, in order to have the faith to make it through the wilderness.

This is a symbolic representation of how we create idols and turn to them in this day and age. When we think that God, our Leader, has abandoned us, then we turn to anything to become our god. I turned to so many other things instead of turning to Jesus, because it was the only thing I had ever relied on and in a sense, trusted, to alleviate my pain.

When we turn to idols, we close ourselves off to the power of God and turn away from His ability to help us, even in our darkest hour. Even after I came to know Christ, I still turned away from Him, because the other idols that I had turned to for so many years were familiar to me.

As human beings, we tend to turn to the familiar, rather than what is good for us. We turn to alcohol, sex, drugs, pornography, food, exercise, work and many other things in order to comfort our pain, fill our loneliness, or bring us a sense of worthiness. I tried every one of those things and turned to them for years, but nothing worked. In fact, my cycle of destruction only got worse as I turned to these things time and time again.

We are to put away every idol. Colossians 3:5 NKJV says, "Therefore put to death your members which are on the earth: fornication, uncleanness, passion, evil desire, and covetousness, which are idolatry." I repented for bowing down to these idols and fully turn back to God once and for all. "Therefore, my beloved, flee from idolatry" (1 Corinthians 10:14 NKJV). God wants to fulfill our every need and be the One that we turn to at every disappointment and victory of our lives.

I started to repent for these idols one by one. I had to verbally ask for forgiveness from the Lord for turning to them. Repenting means to truly turn away from something and not go back. I had to be serious about it and take action.

My counselor walked me through this process of repentance. I would say something along the lines of, "Lord, I ask for Your forgiveness for turning to alcohol to alleviate my pain. Your Word says, 'And my God shall supply all your needs according to His riches in glory by Christ Jesus.' I believe this scripture, so today I repent from turning to anything other than You to fulfill my every need. Lord, please help me turn to You in my weakness, every time I experience hard times and disappointment. Fill me up to overflowing with Your love and joy. Amen" (Philippians 4:19 NKJV).

I went through every idol one by one. It wasn't an overnight success in turning from them. Just like repeating forgiveness over and over when I was feeling angry, I had to repent over and over every time I turned back to an idol. Slowly and surely, I made it out of the fire and back into His arms.

Psalm 37:4 NKJV says, "Delight yourself also in the LORD, and He shall give you the desires of your heart." When I made it to this place of putting the Lord first in my life, I would begin to see many of my desires fulfilled, including a certain man coming back into my life. I was about to see the fullness of a story that only God could write.

Chapter 10

Alive: "vibrant; awake; energetic; filled with vigor"

The final step in my inner healing venture was going to be a process. I had to walk out everything I'd learned in my counseling sessions, utilizing the tools I had developed. We are all presented with choices and we have to choose the right path, as hard as it is. Moving forward in my life as a strong, healthy woman, one who would no longer making destructive choices, was not going to happen overnight. It would be a journey for the days, weeks, months and years ahead.

Within the next year after regularly meeting with my counselor and walking through the steps to inner healing, I stepped back into ministry. I went back to working for the purity ministry for girls and women that I had originally started with. Once again, God's grace abounded in my life.

Despite all of the horrible choices I made along the way, the story of my walk with God in overcoming self-destructive behavior and abuse was stronger than ever before. I was blessed to be able to travel the country and share my testimony with thousands of young girls and their mothers. As it had been all those years before, many would come up to me after the events in tears, thanking me for sharing my story and telling me how encouraging it was for them.

Everything that I had gone through and experienced was being turned around for good. I was able to help others get through their pain, particularly in the areas of sexual abuse and eating disorders. I was finally seeing the exchange of "beauty for ashes" (Isaiah 61:3).

The beauty of this new season continued when I traveled to Mozambique on a missions' trip in 2012. Ever since I was a little girl, I dreamed of going to Africa and work with orphans. God opened a door for that to happen and it was a dream come true.

Our team flew to Johannesburg, changed planes and got on a puddle jumper to Pemba. I gazed out the window over the vast African landscape with tears rolling down my cheeks. God had remembered my hopes and dreams from my childhood and was bringing them to fruition some 30 years later. The presence of God engulfed me as I sat in that airplane seat. He reminded me, "For I know the thoughts that I think toward you, says the Lord, thoughts of peace and not of evil, to give you a hope and a future. Then you will call upon Me and go and pray to Me, and I will listen to you." (Jer. 29:11 NKJV).

Mozambique was hot and dusty. Electricity was running intermittently. We slept with mosquito tents over our beds at night, which protected us from bites and possible malaria. The toilets were latrines. Showers were hit and miss depending on whether the water was turned on or not. If we got in early enough, we might be able to get a weak stream to sprinkle on your body just enough to feel clean and refreshed in the humidity. Every meal consisted of only rice and beans. Needless to say, it was a long way from the comforts of America. The experience opened my eyes to how the majority of the world lives in poverty.

Our dorms were on the same compound as the orphanage. When we woke up in the morning and walked to breakfast, they were waiting to greet us and give us big hugs. Compared to America, it was like night and day. These children were so ready to be loved and ran to us with open arms in order to receive what we had to give.

We would attend worship services and toddlers we had never met crawled into our laps for cuddles. My motherly instincts instantly came to the surface of my heart. I wanted to give each and every one of these precious ones as much love as I had to give.

I was given the opportunity to speak to a group of teenage girls about purity and inner healing. Many of the girls had come out of situations where they were molested and raped at a young age. I shared my story of overcoming rape, the self-destruction that had ensued, and the process of inner healing I had gone through. I taught about lies, identity, and forgiveness. God was using all of the ugly parts of my life and turning it all around for good, just as I had hoped for all those years ago when I stood in Manhattan on September 11th.

A few days after we arrived, our group piled into jeeps and traveled several hours out into "the bush," a remote village to do outreach. We pitched our tents and settled ourselves in the dirt. It was here on one dark night we showed a Jesus movie that shared the gospel. The team had brought a screen, a projector, and a generator out to show the villagers. Afterwards, I shared my testimony to a group of a hundred or more locals about Christ and what He had done in my life. I spoke about how I had once been suicidal and now I was free. I shared the gospel, how Jesus died on the cross for our sins and rose again, conquering death, so that we could have life in abundance. I told them that I am not perfect, that I still stumble, but that He has given me hope.

Many gave their lives to the Lord that night. This night, this missions' trip, made everything that I had gone through worth it just so I could lead them to salvation. It was one of the most rewarding experiences of my life. I was walking out my destiny as God had intended it to be.

I returned back to the states filled with passion to continually be used by God for His plans and purposes. More amazing opportunities were waiting for me when I arrived. I attended a discipleship school where I met amazing friends and received even more inner healing. I was also able to pick up right where I had left off with acting and on-camera work. This time I worked more consistently than I ever had before. It was really fulfilling to be booking commercials and hosting work regularly after so many years of auditioning. I could officially call myself a working actor again, while simultaneously having a firm footing in Christ.

Inner healing delivered me into a healthy life, but it wasn't perfect. I'd like to say that I was completely renewed in my thinking and behavior after that intense season of working with my counselor, but I was not. The devil was always waiting there to try and bring me back into my old sinful ways. There were times when I would briefly step back into the self-destructive behavior that had dominated my life for so many years. I started drinking sporadically after 2 years of sobriety. I'd go out and drink with friends in times of loneliness or disappointment, as I always had.

I was also perpetually single, so when I would go out on dates with men, I'd also thought I could have a drink or two. Once again, I thought I could handle it, but truth be told, sometimes I could and other times I couldn't. Those "other" times were the problem. After just one drink, I would say and do things that represented the old Simone. It was clear: alcohol was, and always has been, a gateway for me to slide back into sin.

I take heart in knowing that not even Jesus was immune to temptation by Satan. "And the devil said to Him, 'If You are the Son of God, command this stone to become bread.' But Jesus answered Him, saying, 'It is written, 'Man shall not live by bread alone, but by every word of God'" (Luke 4:3-4). He was tempted three times in this passage of scripture and every time, He combated the temptation with truth from the Word of God. The interesting part about this is that scripture says, "Now when the devil had ended every temptation, he departed from

Him until an opportune time" (Luke 4:13 NKJV). The devil presented Jesus with every temptation and when that didn't work, he left him until a more opportune time. As it was with me.

It was clear that the devil was not going to quit trying to lure me back into sin. But just like Jesus did in that passage and from what I had learned in the inner healing process, I identified lies and spoke out truth. The key to victory was to identify the lies and the triggers and recognize my behavior. With the tools that I had learned, I was consistently walking with God again.

I'm reminded of a toddler who has a very long season of learning how to walk. I was the baby who kept taking a few steps and then falling again, over and over. I knew the mechanics of walking with Christ, but when I took my eyes off of Him, I would fall. Apostle Peter walked on water while staring at Jesus, but as soon as he looked away, he sank. That was me.

Now I also had all of the inner healing tools and I used them over and over again. The more I applied them and dove into God, the longer and farther I walked in health. I was truly seeing a difference in my life. When I would start to be pulled into the direction of old behaviors, I would read the Bible, pray, spend time with friends and mentors, and have them pray for me. I pressed into Jesus even in times when I didn't feel His presence. It was the combination of these actions that kept me free. I finally had the tools to keep myself in a solid place with the Lord in my life. For the most part, the cycle of destruction was broken.

Now that I was on solid footing spiritually, I felt like I could freely move into the plans and purposes God had for me. It was a new time in my life. I was turning forty years old and there were some things I had always wanted to do and accomplish. In many ways, I felt like the first forty years of my life were just a warm-up and I was ready to tackle the next forty with all the passion and gusto that I had within me. I started setting goals and checking them off of my list one by one.

I'd always been a very determined person and the new decade was proving no different. I was involved in a church community and had my acting career, which was great, but deep down I felt a lack of fulfillment. I had a gnawing in my belly and I yearned for something more. There were so many things that I wanted to do that I never got around to doing because I was dealing with so much junk over the years. I wanted to push myself in ways I had never pushed myself before and I didn't want to look back on my life and regret that I never got around to accomplishing or experiencing those dreams on my "to do" list.

I was still single, which seemed like it was dragging on for ages. I didn't have a partner to walk with me through life, which was tough since I had watched so many people in my life get married. It was really exhausting to be alone sometimes, but if there was ever a time to go after these dreams, it was while I was single, so I just went for it.

I got out of LA. Again. This time to a new place I had never been: Phoenix. I'd bounced around so much in my life, from city to city, but each time I moved and settled down in different places, my life was impacted in different ways. I desperately wanted a slower pace of life. In LA, I was auditioning and working non-stop, and with the increase of the cost of living in Southern California, I felt like I was on a treadmill of financial instability on which I was working to live, rather than living to work. The life of an actor had always been up and down financially and emotionally. I wanted stability. And first and foremost, I wanted to go after some of those long-lost dreams that had collected dust over the years.

Arizona gave me the time and financial resources to tackle these goals. I wrote the first draft of this book, shot a commercial, produced, directed and hosted my own travel show, learned how to ride a motorcycle, and took sommelier courses to become a wine expert, all shortly after I moved there. I was a woman who had been unleashed into her dreams.

One of the goals I'd had all those years ago as a teenager was competing in a fitness competition. After my figure skating career was over, I had been searching for a sport to compete in, and as I had mentioned previously, bodybuilding fitness competitions were all the rage in the 90's. I'd been working out in the gym and lifting weights all through my teen years and it seemed like a perfect sport for me to compete. However, given everything I was dealing with during those years– the rape, the depression, the eating disorder– I was never able to make it happen.

In the decades to follow, I was never in an emotionally or physically healthy place to compete. But after twenty-five years, the desire still had not left. I wanted to find out how strong I could be, what my potential was, and how God had really designed my body. And now that I was in my forties, I had even more incentive.

The competitive spirit that I'd always had endured. I didn't want to enter what most call "middle age" with average physical health. I wanted to crush the second half of my life with the most fit body I could possibly achieve. With my body image issues dealt with and several of my emotional wounds healed, my focus had shifted from how I looked on the outside to how healthy I was on the inside.

After I renounced the lies surrounding my body image and repented of the idol of being thin, I noticed that I was happier with my body and my appearance. I didn't want to starve myself but wanted to be healthy and treat my body well. I was in a solid place in my life to enter a fitness competition, just like I had wanted to do as a teenager.

I jumped full force into transforming my forty-one year old body into a fitness competitor. It seems like an oxymoron for someone who had been so obsessed with her weight for so many years, but it was because I had gone through a ring of fire with my body image that I wanted to challenge myself.

This time, my body transformation was about strength and determination. I wanted to see how strong I could possibly become and test the limits of God's creation within my body. It was a spiritual journey of being healed in the area of body image. If I could get through this competition without being negatively obsessed with my body, and without body dysmorphia, it would be a sign that I was healed of my eating disorder. I was committed to accomplishing this goal.

It was during the time I was training that I had several dreams about the man I had been in a year long relationship with years earlier, who I had loved deeply, but who Jesus had me walk away from. It was Troy. He hadn't been on my mind for years. However, in my dreams at night, we got back into a relationship. Several times I woke up in the morning crying from happiness.

Seven years had passed since I had broken up with him. I had thought about him a few times, but never wanted or yearned for him since. I decided enough time had passed that I could reach out to him on Facebook and say hello. He wrote back and we started corresponding sporadically. At the time, we were both dating other people, so I don't think either of us were thinking that we would ever get back together. However, our little conversations via social media continued until we met up while I was back in LA visiting for an audition.

I arrived at the restaurant before he did. I was nervous. I hadn't seen this man in seven years. Questions ran through my mind. Would he still be mad at me for breaking up with him? Would he start to like me again? Would we have anything to talk about? Would he be the same? What did he look like now? I was nervous and excited all at once.

When he walked into the restaurant, I looked up and thought to myself, "Wow, he has aged just like George Clooney!" He was so handsome, fit, healthy, striking, and the most noticeable trait, he had a gentler demeanor about him, like he had gotten softer with age.

We could barely get a word in edgewise with each other as we caught up with the years, telling each other about the time that had passed. I finally got around to asking him for forgiveness for hurting him when I walked out of his life. He said that he had understood why I did it and forgave me. He told me that God had been working in his life, how he was listening to sermons, reading the Bible and pressing into knowing more about Him. What? The guy who didn't want to follow God while we were dating? The one the Lord had me walk away from?

It was clear that something had shifted in him. He saw the world through different lenses than he had when I knew him seven years prior. When he talked about the Lord, he was soft and tender. He was changed. I recognized this shift, because God had done this in my own life. And now I saw that He had drawn this man towards Him during the years we were apart.

That night, something in my heart felt the same way it used to feel, in all the right ways. Troy felt safe and comfortable for me. It was peaceful and gentle. But moreover, he was pursuing God.

My mind was blown. When I got back to Phoenix, I returned to my life, but we kept communicating in the days and weeks afterwards. I couldn't stop thinking about him. I realized that he was the only man who had ever really loved me with honor and respect, the way I knew I was supposed to be loved.

One day we were texting and I jokingly said, "Come to Phoenix to visit!" Then suddenly I thought, "Oh no! What did I just do?" Questions plagued me: If the Lord had led me away from Troy in 2009, did He still want me to stay away from him after all these years? Was spending time with Troy what He wanted? Was I being disobedient? Was I acting out of the loneliness of being single? Was I pining for what was familiar? I prayed all through it, but ultimately, I couldn't overthink it. I just had to trust that God would lead me in the right direction, whatever that was. So, seven years after our break-up, Troy came to visit me over Fourth of July weekend 2016. I decided that I was just going to spend time with him as friends and see what God had in store.

The weekend arrived and Troy landed in Phoenix. It was awkward at first, but shortly afterwards, it was the same comfort that I always knew with him. Again, I felt that wave of safety come over me with him. I trusted him.

We spent endless hours talking, of God, and what He was doing in our lives. We also talked about our break-up, why I left, and what happened afterwards. It was truly like old friends were catching up and fitting pieces of a puzzle together that were lost in the years gone by. We kept our distance from each other physically, while we reconnected mentally and emotionally. It was an amazing weekend filled with fun and laughter.

When he flew back to LA, I had some serious conversations with the Lord and with my closest friends, who I had trusted time and again in my life. I didn't want to get into yet another relationship that wasn't His best for me, let alone one that He had taken me out of years earlier. But as time went on, I longed for Troy and felt the stirring of love for him in my heart again. I told him that I was missing him, so he came back to visit me again just two weeks later.

While I was busy living my life for the Lord, pursuing all kinds of dreams and goals I had always wanted to accomplish, even settling down in another state, here he was, walking back into my life. I told the Lord, "Look, if we get back together again, that's it. I am not going to break his heart again nor have to recover from a broken one myself."

I prayed and I had those trusted friends and mentors pray. But nobody could deny how perfect it was for us to come back together after all those years during which God had worked on both of our hearts. I also felt the Lord's peace in the idea of us getting back together.

The next time he came to visit, it was no longer a platonic friendship of getting to know each other. It was romantic. I felt all those feelings of falling in love with someone, but better because I knew this man, we had a history together. We had candle lit dinners, held hands, and he wrapped his large arms around me. We talked for hours about God and what we both wanted in our lives. It took all of those years for God to lead us around and teach us His ways separately, and then bring us full circle back together again. It was like I was home again.

Just before he returned to Los Angeles, he told me that he was falling in love with me again. I felt the same way. I knew that if I were to decide to get back into this relationship again, it would be for good. I prayed about it and sensed Holy Spirit saying "Yes" to our relationship. My friends, who had walked through the last eight years with me, also felt that this was what God intended.

We knew it was right, so that was it. Seven months later, after seven years apart, on the seventeenth day of the month, on his forty-seventh birthday, we were married. After all those years alone, after all of that heartache, after all of that wrestling, struggling, tears and abuse, I stood before the only man I had ever truly loved, the only man who ever treated me as I believe Jesus treats His bride, the church, and pledged to be his wife.

God had changed both of our hearts over the course of those seven years. I needed to go through all of that inner healing and accomplish many of those dreams before we got back together. Troy also had to go through his own healing, his battle with addiction, the loss of both of his parents, and then turn to God.

After all those years of pain and turmoil, God brought back to me the man He had called me to leave, a man who loved me with all he had, who honored me, who considered me the apple of his eye. God brought me a man who I feel safe and protected with, one who puts his arms around me when I am broken, in tears, who boasts about my accomplishments to others with a gleam in his eye, and ultimately, a man who treats me as Jesus would want me to be treated.

Oh, and that fitness competition? I got into the best shape of my life, won my division, and placed third overall with women who were half my age. During the training process, Holy Spirit taught me about becoming stronger in Him, about training to be a warrior for Christ. My weightlifting became an outward sign of what God was doing inside of me, making me into a solid rock. Time at the gym was spent listening to sermons and podcasts, reading books and praying, all while working out.

I learned that there is so much more life that God has for me to live. Even though I am in my forties, I'm healthier and more fit, both spiritually and physically than I have ever been in my whole life. At every turn, at every victory, I was learning that all things really are possible in Christ Jesus who strengthens me (Philippians 4:13). My mission is to inspire and teach others to go after their dreams too, whether it be in fitness, health, ministry, acting, business, or other life goals.

Chapter 11

Summit: "zenith; highest point on a mountaintop; mountain peak"

I lived my life as a little rugged girl before I was raped, bold and brash, going after everything I wanted without fear. After I was raped, I was thrust into womanhood, having to deal with adult issues of pain and self-destructive behavior. I spent years pressing, scraping, clamoring, and pushing towards healing and peace. The rugged woman I had become longed to be that carefree rugged girl again.

I have countless photos on my social media of hiking. They're usually taken at the top of a mountain because who takes a picture on the trail? These photos represent victory for me. I cherish them. However, these mountain top photos miss the scenery along the way, the journey to get there. What is along the trail is just as important as the view from the top. After the long hike is over, our bodies feel exhausted but amazing, having been pushed to the limit. We celebrate with a huge meal and a long sleep and wake up to plan the next time we get to go on a beautiful hike. Well, at least I do.

When I started writing this book in 2015, I didn't know what my ending would look like. I joked, "Watch, it will probably end with me getting married." And it did. I had to completely rewrite this book in 2019 in order to better explain the journey from the perspective of where I have ended up, at least for now. When we are going through tough times, we can never see the outcome clearly. It's only when we get on the other side of the turmoil that hindsight is 20/20.

God took a girl who had been raped at fourteen, who allowed herself to be sexually abused for more than half of her life, starved her body, hated herself, and so much more, then brought all things together for good for her, just the way Romans 8:28 puts it: "And we know that all things work together for good to those who love God, to those who are called according to His purpose."

There was one last detail that needed to be dealt with before I moved on to the next chapter of my life. I'd quit drinking for a couple of years after the end of my engagement to Jonah but had picked it back up again sporadically. Even though I had issues with it for so many years, I didn't think that it would be a struggle after walking through inner healing and getting married to Troy. I thought that because I had dealt with the root issues of why I was drinking, then I wouldn't have a problem anymore. However, even though I was no longer turning to alcohol to escape depression and sadness, I had started to turn to it for other reasons.

There is a scripture in Song of Solomon which reads, "Catch us the foxes, the little foxes that spoil the vines, for our vines have tender grapes." (Song of Solomon 2:15 NKJV). The "tender grapes" were the fruit of my life in Christ and all of the beautiful opportunities that He had blessed me with, like being a national speaker or doing mission's work in Africa. I was supposed to be enjoying my life and advancing His Kingdom, but the foxes were those things that crept in when I wasn't looking, that sought to destroy that fruit. For me, alcohol was one of them.

We live in a society where alcohol is pervasive. Wine tasting, craft beers, and handcrafted cocktails have become a part of our culture. I had also grown to love the differences in flavors and textures of alcohol, just as a food connoisseur is passionate about trying different cuisines. I'd even passed a wine sommelier exam and had started to enjoy the taste of various whiskey and gin. It had returned to my life as a casual enjoyment, a social activity, or a token of reward at the end of a long day. But it progressively got worse.

As I was getting older, I wasn't drinking with the intention to get drunk, just to feel light-hearted and take the "edge off" life's day-to-day stresses. I tend to be a very serious person, so alcohol gave me that sense of lightening my load and relaxation. As goal oriented as I am, it was also a way for me to forget about those things I was laser focused on achieving and just kick back. I had begun to associate alcohol with "having fun" and when I started to feel good, I would want to feel even better, which would lead to the next drink.

When I was training for the fitness competition, I was in the gym six days per week. My diet was tightened up to counting every macronutrient I was consuming. When Troy and I would go out on a date, we would have drinks, so I could have one night of "relaxation" from my goal of getting into the best shape of my life. But even though I was in competition prep, I would still get drunk and get back in the gym the next day to work even harder than before to accomplish my vision.

I also started to believe that I was not good at socializing. It became a crutch to loosen me up while I was out with friends or co-workers. This was a new lie that had crept in over the years. Naturally, I lean towards being introverted, which is strange, because I'm a performer. However, I'm someone who recharges by being alone, so if I had a choice of what to do at night, I'd typically stay home and read a book or watch a documentary. I would get out of practice communicating with others and feel awkward in social situations. Thus, an old lie was birthed, but this time it had a twist: "you're not good enough in social situations".

I'm learning that new lies will always come, but it is how we react to them that will change the course of our destinies. I reacted to this one by drinking more. Sometimes I could have one or two and other times, I would blackout. I'd never be able to predict what was going to happen when I drank. I always thought I would be able to handle it and then it would sneak up on me. My intake was unpredictable. I was all over the place with it. Even after one drink, I did not make rational decisions, which was dangerous.

While I was writing this book, I had one of those nights. I went to a brewery to have a couple of beers with my Dad. I love hanging out with him. It is one of my favorite things to do. It bonded us, just like I had wanted over the years. That afternoon we told stories, reminisced, and laughed. It was my special father-daughter time.

We met some other people and struck up a conversation. I'd been working so hard on my business endeavors that I hadn't been socializing very much. It felt so good to get out and meet new people, something I don't do on a regular basis.

My Dad ended up leaving and going home, but I chose to stay behind. I continued talking and laughing with this couple when they bought me another beer. It was after that one that I couldn't remember what happened next. What was meant to be going out for a quick beer or two on a relaxing afternoon, ended up with me drunk, getting behind the wheel of my brand-new dream car. Once again, I could hardly believe what I had done. I was disgusted with myself. I didn't even think about calling a cab or calling my Dad to pick me up, because I simply didn't know what I was doing.

That night, once again, after the countless times over the course of my life, driving home drunk and other reckless behavior, I made it home safely. I did not get pulled over by police, nor did I get into an accident or kill someone. Any one of these scenarios had been possible. Yet once again, I made it. When I sobered up, I thought to myself, how many times would this have to happen to me for me to learn my lesson? Even though I had repented of it during my inner healing sessions, it was reintroduced to me through a new lie. This was clearly an idol, which had also become an addiction.

I had to take an inventory of my life and be realistic about what exactly was happening with my relationship with alcohol. What I knew, but did not want to admit, was that I had started to crave it. The best way to describe this is how the body desires sugar or anything else that causes a physiological response to make us feel good. My body would literally get excited at the thought of having a drink. Sometimes, I'd count the hours until I could have one. At times, my drinking had progressed to me coming home every night and drinking until I fell asleep. This had gone beyond just consuming alcohol in social situations. I was going to have to make a choice: continue drinking and risk my life, which I had fought so long to keep, or work towards putting alcohol into the grave once and for all. This was my new rock bottom.

I have realized that I am an alcoholic. People have refuted me on this, because I am not your "wake up and drink a fifth of vodka" kind of girl. Alcohol addictions come in all shapes and sizes. It runs in my family and I'd been drinking since the age of 12. I was able to stop for brief periods of time and go back to it, thinking that I could control it. I couldn't. If I was going to make lasting changes, I had to be honest with myself and make a clear choice: keep drinking and losing my life or fight the battle until it was won.

When a military goes to war, they gain victory from overcoming a series of smaller battles. I had countless battles with alcohol over a 30-year period and it was time for me to assume the victory for good. This was ultimately a battle with Satan over my life. It is the one idol I have turned back to time and again and was now an addiction. It is something I need to work on consistently, because the temptation to drink creeps up on me unexpectedly. "Watch and pray, lest you enter into temptation. The spirit is indeed willing, but the flesh is weak." (Matt. 26:41 NKJV).

I am now sober.

My story is one of God's redeeming love. I love this definition of redeem: "To gain or regain possession of (something) in exchange for payment" (Oxford). That is exactly what Jesus did on the cross. This is what Jesus died for. He died on the cross for our freedom, so we could be free from the devil's bondage's, free from sin, free from depression and oppression. He gave His life as payment so that we could gain life back again.

When I gave my heart to Christ, my redemption was technically instant, but it has been a process of me walking it out, learning, and struggling to get to the other side of freedom. But I did it with Him. We all have to do that. We all want to (and dare I say have to) get onto the other side of the difficulty into freedom.

He's given us the Bible as a tool to use throughout our lives. Freedom does not just happen at salvation. It's a process of walking out our faith, learning His ways, and pressing in closely to Him. He walks you through it, so that not only do you have amazing blessings on the other side (like winning a fitness competition or getting married), but moreover, so that you are also more Christ-like.

Am I completely free from sin after marriage? Certainly not. I battle daily to keep my walk straight with the Lord with my husband by my side doing the same.

I'm not going to close this book with a "fairytale" ending, but this story is God's glory. In many ways, now that I am married, it is another new beginning where I have to learn a whole new set of tools to use to walk out this new season. Marriage continues to further challenge and smooth out the rough edges of my personality and the behaviors that stem from my past.

Within the last couple of years, I encountered an experience that had me go through a familiar battle. I had wanted a particular on-camera job for eight years. This job echoed everything that Simone embodied as a child. I got to be fun, playful and, essentially, "sell products in the mirror," like I did when I was a kid. It was such a breath of fresh air after all I had been through over the years for God to be bringing this back around into my life. I felt like that little girl every time I was in front of that camera.

I first auditioned for this job in 2010 and auditioned for it five times over the course of eight years. Two of those times I made it down to the final ten out of 10,000 applicants who auditioned. The odds of me being so close so many times in a row were rare at best. So, when it came around again recently, I fully believed that I would book this dream job.

I had worked my butt off to prepare. I had researched, practiced, and got private coaching. I laid my heart out before the Lord in the weeks leading up to the audition and callback. I fasted, I prayed, and I worshiped. This was a job that I felt I was born to do and He was opening up the door for it yet again in my life. He deserves all of the praise. He knows me so deeply and is so wonderful that He would bless me with this opportunity. Through all of it, I believed the Lord was leading me towards it.

I walked into the audition room with couches full of executives and was the same Simone who was childlike, fun, and free, just like I had been back in the 80's before my life took a turn. I stepped before them vulnerable, but prepared. I wasn't perfect, but I was authentically myself. This was the little girl who was silly and quirky little girl. Everything that God created me to be. In many ways, I was that short haired twelve-year old wearing that Opus sweatshirt walking back into that arcade hoping that I would be picked.

I felt good about my audition, not great, because I tend to be very technical, but I trusted that God would work out the rest. He picks up for us where we leave off. And there was nothing more I could have done to get ready for the audition than I did. I'd given it my all.

For the next two weeks, I waited with baited-breath. Then I got the call from my agent. She told me that they said no to me, that I needed to move on, because this was the end of the road for me with this job. I'd been going after it for eight years and this was their final decision. I was crushed.

I had been in the entertainment industry for more than twenty years and had believed that this was my moment for my breakthrough on-camera job. I thought this was the time when it was going to finally happen for me, now that I am married with my husband by my side, and in a solid place with the Lord. Then pow, right in the kisser.

I was devastated. I felt rejected. All of those thoughts and old feelings came bubbling up inside of me. The lies started bombarding me again: I'm not good enough, I'm too old (new one now that I'm in my forties), I didn't do well in my audition, they didn't like me, God didn't come through for me, and on and on. I started to spiral down this dark hole of lies and negative thoughts. I wanted to drink, I wanted to starve myself, I wanted to go back to old ways of coping with disappointment. I cried tears of sorrow from the depths of my gut as my husband held me in his arms.

Two days after I heard the news, I woke up in the morning and went to spend time with the Lord in my journal and in the Bible. I felt numb and depressed. I was desperate for Him to speak to me that morning, so I asked Him where in the Word I should read. It was almost an instant response: Proverbs 15. I read a few verses until I came across the one that jumped off the page. It read, "Everything seems to go wrong when you feel weak and depressed. But when you choose to be cheerful, every day will bring you more and more joy and fullness" (Proverbs 15:15 TPT). It hit me like a ton of bricks. I didn't have to slide down into this hole of depression and could choose to be cheerful.

All of the sudden, it was as clear as day to me: the enemy had tried to use this disappointment to cause me to spiral back down into old ways of thinking and unhealthy patterns, but I was not going to let him. I was done being his pawn, and I was determined to bring something beautiful out of my heartache. A strength rose up in me and, using the principles I've written about in this book, I got myself out of the cycle of lies that were trying to entangle me. I chose the right way.

Inner healing isn't a "one and done" sort of deal. It's a journey. We fall because we're human beings. Jesus died to cover that. Holy Spirit is there to pick us back up, dust us off, and set us back out, marching us on our way again, like a kid learning how to ride a bike. A seasoned athlete still has times when he or she makes mistakes and falls, but the winner is the one who gets back up and keeps going. Have you ever watched the CrossFit Games? If not, I encourage you to watch some footage of these athletes. Talk about rugged determination and persistence to never quit. That is what I want to carry in my walk with the Lord.

We can do all of the inner healing work, but ultimately, we all have choices to make. I had a choice that day, to go back down the road of destruction or to go down the road of life. We will be tested again. The devil will always be beckoning us to walk down the dark road and if he's not, he's just waiting for a more "opportune time." The final step of inner healing is to take everything that you have learned and put it into action. Make the right choices given the tools that God has given you in His Word.

I'm writing this book so that you will know that you too can be healed, you can make the right choices, you can be set free. It's an ongoing process, but it is possible. Christ died for us to have it. He didn't die for us to have depressed and miserable lives always falling short of our hopes and dreams. No, He died so that we could have life. "But I have come to give you everything in abundance, more than you expect–life in its fullness until you overflow!" (John 10:10 TPT).

I recently shared my testimony with someone I had just met. He said, "When I look at you, I see such a solid and secure woman of God. It's so hard to believe that you went through all of that and came out so confident in who you are on the other side." See, the man who was saying this was only looking at the picture of me "on the mountaintop," but he wasn't seeing what it took to get me there on that dusty, dirty, rocky trail. He didn't see the sweat and tears and near-death exhaustion. He only saw the woman who was standing before him that day. So, I responded to him, "It's all God." He gave me every tool to make it up to the mountaintop that I am standing on today.

But the journey isn't over. Remember how I hiked with my parents in the mountains as a child? Forty years later, we are still hiking together. I am now forty-five and they are seventy-nine, but every time

I'm up there I feel like the little girl again, rugged and determined, carefree with a lightness of being. When we are out in the high peaks of the Sierra Mountains of California, I am reminded of the paths that God has all of us walking on.

Our lives are like climbing up to one mountain peak and looking into the distance, only to see many more peaks lying before us. We relish the view from where we are standing, but also come to the realization that we have many more yet to climb. From there we must continue forging ahead so we can get to our destination, and all the way along the landscape is stunning and breathtaking (literally in high altitude).

This is where I stand today, on top of one peak, looking ahead. The strength and wisdom I gained in the first half of my life has prepared me for the second half. After walking through the inner healing, laying down alcohol, surrendering my life to Christ again and again, I'm fit to continue onto and into whatever the Lord has waiting for me next.

At the end of my hikes, my desire for my physical destination on this earth after a hike is my warm flannel jammies and hot food in my belly beside my parents and my husband. My life-long spiritual destination is to be in Heaven is being filled with the love of Jesus, resting in His arms forever. Therefore, I press on, fighting the good fight of faith (1 Timothy 6:12), alongside the Father, the Son and the Holy Spirit.

References

"rugged." *Merriam-Webster.com*. Merriam-Webster, 2019. Web. https://www.merriam-webster.com/dictionary/rugged (28 October 2019)

"violated." *Merriam-Webster.com*. Merriam-Webster, 2020. Web. https://www.merriam-webster.com/dictionary/violate (30 January 2020)

"renounce." *Merriam-Webster.com*. Merriam-Webster, 2020. Web. https://www.merriam-webster.com/dictionary/renounce (29 January 2020)

"metamorphosis." *Merriam-Webster.com*. Merriam-Webster, 2020. Web. https://www.merriam-webster.com/dictionary/metamorphosis (30 January 2020)

"tumbling (tumble)." *Merriam-Webster.com*. Merriam-Webster, 2020. Web. https://www.merriam-webster.com/dictionary/tumble (30 January 2020)

"engaged (engage)." *Merriam-Webster.com*. Merriam-Webster, 2020. Web. https://www.merriam-webster.com/dictionary/engage (30 January 2020) "healing (heal)." *Merriam-Webster.com*. Merriam-Webster, 2020. Web. https://www.merriam-webster.com/dictionary/heal (30 January 2020)

"idol." From Google. Oxford, 2019.
Web. https://www.lexico.com/en/definition/idol (28 October 2019)

"deliverance." From Google. Oxford. 2020.
Web. *https://www.lexico.com/definition/deliverance* (29 January 2020)

"identity." From Google. Oxford. 2020.
Web. *https://www.lexico.com/definition/identity* (29 January 2020)

"redeem." From Google. Oxford. 2020.
Web. *https://www.lexico.com/definition/identity* (30 January 2020)

Wikipedia contributors. (2019, November 10). Statutory rape. In *Wikipedia, The Free Encyclopedia*. Retrieved 1:04pm, November 15, 2019, from
https://en.wikipedia.org/w/index.php?title=Statutory_rape&oldid=925544032